The
Terrier
Handbook

Kerry V. Kern

Filled with Full-color Photographs
Illustrations by Michele Earle-Bridges

BARRON'S

About the Author

Kerry V. Kern is the author of eight books on dog breeds, including Labrador Retrievers, Siberian Huskies, and Rottweilers, all in Barron's *Complete Pet Owner's Manual* series. She worked as editor of *The Canine Graphic,* was senior editor at *Congressional Quarterly Press,* and was a member of the Dog Writers Association of America.

Cover Photos

Front cover: Tara Darling/Parson Russell Terrier (left), Bull Terrier (top center), Bedlington Terrier (bottom right), Pets by Paulette/Cairn Terrier (bottom center), West Highland White Terriers (top right), Yorkshire Terrier (middle right).
 Inside front cover: Tara Darling/Parson Russell Terrier
 Inside back cover: Pets by Paulette/Cairn Terriers
 Back cover: Pets by Paulette/Miniature Schnauzer

Acknowledgments

I am most grateful to the hard-working secretaries of the national clubs for the breeds included in this book. Their cooperation in furnishing requested help and information was invaluable in the development of this edition.

Photo Credits

Norvia Behling: 3, 14, 16, 30, 32, 46, 50, 52, 56, 58, 59, 63, 72, 76, 79, 83, 101. Kent Dannen: 39, 113, 114, 125, 126, 144, 145, 158, 159. Tara Darling: 2, 7, 8, 10, 21, 25, 26, 28, 42, 51, 54, 61, 66, 85, 88, 90 (below), 94, 96, 97, 98, 99, 106, 107, 109, 112, 116 (both photos), 119, 120, 124 (above), 133, 135, 118 (above), 120, 128, 156, 162. Isabelle Francais: 7, 18, 20, 27, 38 (left), 49, 69, 87, 90 (above), 92, 93, 103 (below), 105 (above), 109, 110, 118 (below), 121, 122, 124 (below), 127, 129, 130, 139, 140, 141, 142, 143, 147 (below), 148, 149, 151, 152, 153, 154, 155, 163. Patti Neale: 136, 138. Pets by Paulette: vii, viii, 17, 22, 23, 24, 31, 45, 60, 95, 103 (above), 105 (below), 131, 132, 134, 147 (top), 160. Judith Strom: 38 (right), 64. Connie Summers: 100.

All inquiries should be addressed to:
Barron's Educational Series, Inc.
250 Wireless Boulevard
Hauppauge, New York 11788
www.barronseduc.com

International Standard Book No. 0-7641-2860-4

Library of Congress Catalog Card No. 2004058547

Library of Congress Cataloging-in-Publication Data
Kern, Kerry V.
 The terrier handbook / Kerry V. Kern ; with full-color photographs ; drawings by Michele Earle-Bridges.—2nd ed.
 p. cm.
 Rev. ed. of: The new terrier handbook. c1988.
 Includes index.
 ISBN 0-7641-2860-4
 1. Terriers. I. Kern, Kerry V. New terrier handbook.
 II. Title.

SF429.T3K472 2005
636.755—dc22   2004058547

Printed in China
9 8 7 6 5 4 3 2 1

Important Note

This pet handbook gives advice to the reader about buying and caring for a new dog. The author and publisher consider it important to point out that the advice given in the book applies to normally developed puppies or adult dogs, obtained from recognized dog breeders or adoption shelters—dogs that have been examined and are in excellent health with good temperament.

Anyone who acquires a grown dog should be aware that the animal has already formed its basic impression of human beings and their customs. The new owner should watch the animal carefully, especially its attitude toward humans. If possible, the new owner should meet the former owner before adopting the dog. If the dog is adopted from a shelter, the new owner should make an effort to obtain information about the dog's background, personality, and peculiarities. Dogs that come from abusive homes or from homes in which they have been treated abnormally may react to handling in an unnatural manner, and may have a tendency to snap or bite. Dogs with this nature should only be adopted by people who have had experience with such dogs.

Caution is further advised in the association of children with dogs, both puppies and adults, and in meeting other dogs, whether on or off lead.

Well-behaved and carefully supervised dogs may cause damage to someone else's property or cause accidents. It is therefore in the owner's interest to be adequately insured against such eventualities, and we strongly urge all dog owners to purchase liability policies that cover their dogs.

Contents

Preface

Among the usual classifications of dog breeds—hound, sporting, terrier, toy, working, herding, etc.—I think the terriers have the most distinctive personalities. The breeds that derive from an "earth dog" heritage are often described as feisty, lively, and energetic, but the most common term is "game": a plucky and unyielding spirit, ready and willing for anything. Terriers originally earned their keep by ridding their masters' homes and fields of vermin and small predators, but from this inauspicious beginning emerged a group of dogs with an incredible amount of courage and an unmatched zest for life. With the passage of time, terriers have adapted to new lifestyles and are rarely called upon to perform the services they were originally bred for, but these instincts remain.

The dogs grouped together in this book under the heading of "terrier" encompass more than thirty distinct breeds, varying in size from toys of a few pounds to a "giant" weighing up to eighty pounds. Each breed is unique, but all share common links.

The breeds described here are not limited to those currently assigned to the Terrier Group by the official kennel clubs in the United States and United Kingdom. When I was initially asked to write this book, the publisher requested that I include all breeds that share the "terrier" name and heritage. While I initially dismissed such breeds as the Yorkshire Terrier or the Giant Schnauzer as not belonging in this text, I soon agreed with the logic of including all dogs that share a common heritage.

Although some of the breeds in this book are more accurately "distant cousins" of the Terrier Group members, all earn their place by their instincts and personalities. Physical differences—primarily size—have led some breeds to be placed in other groups. Some fit more properly in the Toy Group, and others are relegated to the Working and Nonsporting Groups; some have moved through the Miscellaneous Class before gaining official recognition. They come from a variety of backgrounds and have a variety of homelands, but the "earth dog" nature remains. The basic terrier temperament and heritage are the unifying factors in this text.

New to this edition are the Black Russian, Cesky, Glen of Imaal, and

Parson Russell Terriers. The Miniature Bull and Toy Fox Terriers received recognition as separate breeds since the first publication of this text and are presented individually.

One breed carrying the "terrier" name, the Tibetan Terrier, is not included. It does not descend from recognized terrier strains, does not have the typical terrier disposition, and does not "go to the earth" as terriers do. This ancient breed received the name "terrier" when it was introduced to the Western world primarily because its size was similar to that of many terriers. A true terrier it is not.

I would like to thank Seymour Weiss, my editor and friend, for his guidance on this project. We go back longer than I care to remember, and he's always given me support and solace whenever needed.

K.V.K.

Chapter One

An Introduction to Terriers

While impossible to document, it is believed that domesticated dogs (*Canis familiaris*) may date back more than 20,000 years. The earliest specimens are thought to have stemmed from ancestors of the wolf family. Both early humans and the forerunners of today's domesticated dog lived a simple existence dominated by the need to hunt to survive. In a mutually satisfactory bond, man supplied all the dog's basic needs and in return the dog aided man in the hunt, in controlling his flocks, and in protecting his home. Over time, man learned how to refine the dog through selective breeding to enhance desired traits. Thus, from these first strains of domestic dog more than 400 distinct breeds have emerged.

Several of the hound breeds have been traced back more than 8,000 years to the time of the pharaohs. Terriers are not nearly as ancient a group, but most can trace their her-

The terriers are tremendously varied in size, type, and color. Their "hard-charging" nature appeals to dog lovers the world over.

itage to the British Isles in the 14th century. Similar breeds were also being developed in Germany around this same time. The word "terrier" is derived from *terra*, the Latin word for "earth." Terriers (literally "earth dogs") were originally used to "go to the ground" and hunt out and destroy small vermin. A terrier trails an animal wherever it may go, often digging down into holes and submerged nests. Controlling vermin required an energetic and courageous animal with a well-developed sense of smell—a dog that could hold its ground against such opponents as foxes, weasels, ferrets, and rats. From the earliest days until modern time, terriers have exhibited courage that belies their moderate size. Pound for pound, there are few breeds that can match the energy, bravery, and stamina of a terrier.

There are more than twenty breeds that formally comprise the Terrier Group, as defined by the American Kennel Club (AKC). There are a number of other breeds that have been assigned to the Toy, Working, and Nonsporting Groups that stem from these early strains of "earthe dogges," as terriers were formerly known.

Most terriers were originally kept by peasants and members of the working class, not as pets but as working dogs to control the pest population. Terriers of all varieties proved to be tireless "ratters" with an innate desire to please and serve their masters. Such loyalty and enthusiasm in time earned such dogs a place in the home as companions as well.

The British Isles are generally regarded as the homeland of most of today's terrier breeds. Because of Britain's varied terrain, terrier breeders were forced to breed their dogs selectively to adapt to the local conditions. Two main groups eventually were established: long-legged and short-legged terriers. The long-legged varieties are generally regarded as the "English" type, with smooth coats, rectangular heads, and erect tails. The short-legged varieties, or the "Scottish" type, typically have a rough coat, a larger head, and a low-slung posture.

Over the years other terrier breeds that did not fit these two classifications also emerged. Some larger, powerfully built terriers were developed to function primarily as fighting breeds in a "sport" long since banned in Britain and the United States. The Staffordshire Bull Terrier and the American Staffordshire Terrier (often referred to as the American Pit Bull Terrier) stem from these lines.

The modern day breeds that trace back to a terrier heritage are:

Airedale Terrier
American Staffordshire Terrier
Australian Terrier
Bedlington Terrier
Black Russian Terrier
Border Terrier
Boston Terrier
Bull Terrier
Cairn Terrier
Dandie Dinmont Terrier
Fox Terrier, Smooth and Wire
Fox Terrier, Toy
Glen of Imaal Terrier
Irish Terrier
Kerry Blue Terrier
Lakeland Terrier
Manchester Terrier, Standard
    and Toy
Norfolk Terrier
Norwich Terrier

Terriers are "earth" dogs that like nothing more than digging into holes and searching for vermin.

Whether alone or in a group, a terrier is interested in everything around it.

Parson Russell Terrier
Schnauzer, Miniature, Standard, and Giant
Scottish Terrier
Sealyham Terrier
Silky Terrier
Skye Terrier
Soft Coated Wheaten Terrier
Staffordshire Bull Terrier
Welsh Terrier
West Highland White Terrier
Yorkshire Terrier

The Evolution of Dogs

The exact origin of the dog is unknown, but some theories place the first doglike animals on earth at around 600,000 B.C. Domesticated dogs are thought to date back about 20,000 years, with their closest recognizable ancestor the wolf. At a time when life was extremely harsh and food supplies limited, these primitive animals learned the benefits of grouping together for survival. Pack behavior developed, with the dogs assuming various ranks within the group. One dog assumed the leadership position, generally through an assertive show of power, and all pack members then worked out their own niche behind the leader.

In earliest times, human and dog competed for the same prey—and human intellect and superior skills ultimately won this contest. Dogs were intelligent enough to recognize, however, the benefits of adaptation to a secondary role as assistant. The dog's ability to subordinate itself to humans while still retaining its spirit has enabled the dog to become our favorite domesticated animal.

Early humans utilized dogs primarily to aid in the hunt for food; as time passed, people learned how to breed dogs selectively to attain certain goals: fast runners, good hunters, avid watchdogs. Such useful qualities served humans well. Over time a bond of friendship also arose and dual-purpose dogs evolved: workers and companions.

Terriers have evolved into a wide variety of types, and ears, tails, and coats have been further modified by human intervention. Typical ear configurations include: (1) folded, (2) cropped, (3) prick, and (4) pendulous.

Behavior Patterns and Their Meaning

While rarely called upon to activate their ancient survival instincts, modern dogs have nevertheless inherited many of the traits utilized by the earliest members of their species. Pack behavior still exists, but in modern times dogs adapt to the *human pack* and the additional demands of rules of civilization. Domestication has done much to temper the aggressive nature of many breeds, but many other characteristics have survived.

Terriers were originally bred to thrive predominantly in hilly territory and keep the terrain clear of predators and small vermin. In other terrains dogs of various structures and temperaments evolved to serve the particular needs of their masters. Even though raised as distinct breeds, they all share a common heritage and basic forms of communication.

Terriers are renowned for their spunky, aggressive nature. This trait is particularly keen in the males. When dog meets dog, there is an immediate vying for dominance. The dogs will stand well up on their feet, snarl, and try to intimidate their perceived opponent. An inspection of the anal area is generally in order. Fierce growling can ensue, and occasionally a fight will break out, but this is usually quite short-lived, as one animal will recognize its vulnerability and give way to the more dominant dog.

The same vying for top spot—the "alpha" dog—will also take place between dog and master, although this is more often a war of wits rather than a physical confrontation. Unless the human clearly asserts leadership, the dog feels it is entitled to rule the pack and will try to do so. Owners should be aware of this trait and exhibit an emphatic, consistent manner when dealing with the dog—especially when it willfully disobeys. The dog must understand that it is subordinate to all humans in its pack, and this instruction should begin as soon as the puppy is introduced into the household. A puppy can comprehend instruction in proper behavior even when quite young, as it has already been coached in this power structure by its mother, the original alpha.

Terriers are very alert, game animals. Despite their instinctive challenge to other animals they feel are vying for superior position, they are not normally prone to viciousness. The atrocities attributed to "pit bull terriers" are actions of poorly bred and improperly raised animals and should not be taken as typical of terrier nature. Owners of the larger, very game terrier breeds (American Staffordshire Terrier, Staffordshire Bull Terrier) have an added responsibility to rigorously attend to the obedience training of their animals. By showing the public the attributes of well-bred, well-trained terriers, some of the ill fame attached to these breeds can be cleared away. As with all breeds, any terrier exhibiting an overly aggressive nature should be thoroughly trained—by a professional if necessary—and eliminated from breeding programs.

Vocalization, Facial Expression, and Posture

Body language and other nonverbal communication are basically uniform among all breeds of dogs—from the mighty Mastiff to the diminutive Chihuahua. An Airedale will instinctively understand the significance of the posturing of the Great Dane, as well as the struts of the Yorkshire. Humans too can learn to interpret these body signs by paying attention to the differences among the various sounds dogs make, and the meaning of the accompanying movements.

A dog at ease will usually have a relaxed posture: the head and ears are up, the tail is at rest. When at attention, the ears point more forward, the tail is more horizontal, and the dog appears more up on its toes. When happy, as when greeting a familiar person, the tail usually moves quickly on a horizontal plane, the ears are up, and the dog may whine or give off some short barks. An upset, aggressive dog will have an angry expression, with its ears either pointed directly forward or lying flat against the side of the head, and it will begin to bare its teeth and emit low, growling tones.

A fearful dog is perhaps the most dangerous, as its agitation is not as apparent as a menacing animal's. It is highly unpredictable. The face is slightly tensed and the ears lie flat to the head; the overall body position is lowered. If the dog feels threatened, it can quickly lash out from this position.

Facial expressions are often keys to a dog's intent. This, however, can be complicated by the length and cut of a breed's coat around the face. Terriers such as the Yorkshires often have much of their face obscured by the lengthy coat, while Bedlingtons are trimmed to make them appear as lambs.

Tails are usually good mood indicators, but many of the terrier breeds have tails that are docked quite short, which makes monitoring the tail positions quite difficult. With dogs that have undocked tails, a horizontal position generally indicates contentment, an upward tail indicates excitement or heightened attention, and a low-slung tail position indicates fear.

Many people improperly interpret a dog's submissive posturing as an indication of guilt by the dog. This is, in fact, merely a resigned response by the dog to an authority more dominant that itself. A submissive dog assumes a lowered position, tail down and tucked under its belly, ears pointing back. It will avoid eye contact. In addition, it may attempt to lick the mouth or hands of the dominant individual. The dog may then roll onto its back or even urinate as further indication of its surrender.

A confused, upset dog may also assume a lowered stance, but it will not grovel or try to lick. Instead, its message is conveyed by rapid panting, indicative of stress.

Body language is highly revealing. By paying attention to your dog's signals, you should be able to assess a situation and make a proper response—such are the actions of a leader in the dog's view.

Communication

Communication with your dog is more than verbal exchanges—commands, praise, and corrections. To help mold your terrier puppy into a well-adjusted adult dog, there are a few basic concepts to bear in mind. A dog will respond to its master according to how it interprets that person's vocal tone and body language. This is all they have to work with. The master must, in turn, show the dog exactly what is expected of it.

Positive experiences teach your dog what you wish it to learn; negative experiences teach fear. A classic example of miscommunication is the following scenario: an owner discovers a housebreaking "mistake" on the carpet, screams in anger, even hits the dog, which is now crouched to the floor and scurrying for safe cover. The owner thinks the dog knows it has done wrong and is showing its guilt. The dog, in fact, is

Terriers love the outdoors and will thrive when given plenty of opportunity to enjoy it.

submitting to the master as a means of self-preservation. It hears and sees the anger and reacts with fear. The dog has not been helped to associate its actions with the master's reactions. This scenario is totally counterproductive; the dog is left confused and the owner has not taken the proper steps toward eliminating further such incidents.

A dog will learn *and retain* information gained from positive experiences. In theory, the learning process is quite simple: An effective leader clearly shows what is expected from the dog, and praises when the task is accomplished. If mistakes are made, the dog is corrected, shown the proper action, and praised when the action is finally completed.

Earth dogs, like this Westie puppy, enjoy nothing more than a good dig.

This simple process can be complicated by many factors. Some terriers are more intelligent, capable learners. Some terriers are quite stubborn and less willing to submit to the will of the master. Some masters are better trainers. Each—dog and teacher—brings an individual set of strengths and weaknesses to the process, and a balance must be struck.

By being alert to what the dog's body language is telling you, and also to what *your* body language and vocal tones are telling the dog, communication can be improved. Your dog has a limited frame of reference, as it must rely on the signals you give with your vocal tones and physical demeanor. If you encounter problems, try to use these cues to help evaluate what the cause may be: Is Rocco testing my authority? Is he confused? Am I making my wishes clear? Can Rocco attain what I am asking of him?

Digging and Burying

Terriers are earth dogs. While all dogs have been known to bury bones and leftover food as a throwback to the ancient times when this aided the dog's survival, this characteristic is deeply ingrained and must be expected in terriers. They love to dig, and many take to it with great fervor. Terriers make great use of their front paws, quickly burrowing deep into the ground, while the rear legs push the discarded dirt neatly (sometimes not so neatly) out the back.

The sheer joy of digging can be an annoyance for the owner. All fencing in the yard should be set to a depth that exceeds the digging capability of the dog, or the fence can be mounted in a solid foundation. Many terriers also display a curious habit of giving a quick dig in the immediate area where they are about to lie down; if this is your hardwood floor or carpeting, there is a problem. This is a throwback to the primitive times when the dog needed to carve out a nest for sleeping in order to protect itself from the elements. A firm, consistently repeated "no" at the instant the dog begins to scratch at the floor should solve this problem.

Most terriers will unhesitatingly enter into open holes or recesses; the possible danger of this is obvious. Do discourage this inclination and admonish the dog for crawling into tight spaces; the best course, however, is prevention. Be sure all old wells and drainage pipes are securely covered and impenetrable. If not, your terrier may take off after its prey—either real or imaginary—and end up wedged or injured.

Chapter Two

Considerations Before You Buy

Selecting a terrier puppy requires more than a decision of which dog or breed is "best." Prospective owners must also take the time to evaluate their lifestyle and the suitability of a dog, specifically a terrier, in their home, as terriers are not for everyone.

Is a Terrier Right for You?

A terrier is an active, often headstrong dog. A good owner must commit to training the dog thoroughly in the basic commands and supplying it with daily love, attention, adequate housing, and an outlet for its energy. Many terrier breeds require a considerable amount of grooming and regular exercise. An owner must make a commitment for the life span of the dog to fulfill its needs, including daily walks for approximately the next 10 to 15 years.

A terrier is by nature strong-willed, with a mind of its own, which means

Investigate the characteristics of the breeds that interest you and how this fits your lifestyle before selecting any terrier.

it might not be a good choice for the first-time dog owner. Without a background in training, a novice owner may experience a good dose of fiery rebellion. Even the smallest terrier is likely to be scrappy, ready to take on adversaries many times its size. This attitude worked well in vermin hunting, but boisterousness might not be appreciated in all homes.

A terrier is generally not a good mix with highly active children, as it may react instinctively and nip. There is an obvious danger of the small terrier being accidentally injured by roughhousing. Many terrier breeders believe that the best age to introduce a terrier to a home is when all children are at least five years old. The Border, the Irish, and the Soft Coated Wheaten Terriers are considered to be very good with children, while most of the other breeds are recommended only for families with older, well-behaved children.

A terrier is generally stronger than it appears, and it will quickly bolt after spotting anything it sees as prey. This eliminates most children from being able to walk the dog on a leash safely. A terrier believes it

If you think you'd enjoy sharing your life with a terrier, be sure that you can meet the requirements of the breed you choose.

belongs in the home, as a family member, so it rarely does well as a yard dog. When outside, it needs to be kept in a securely fenced yard, as it may devise ways to become an escape artist, such as opening gate latches or digging down several feet.

Be sure the breed you select is appropriate for all members of your family. Make certain that a terrier puppy will be welcomed by everyone in the family. Despite good intentions, family members who did not want a dog around may suddenly become "allergic" to it or find it a nuisance. Such situations generally spell disaster for the dog, so think carefully and discuss this acquisition with all involved.

If you do not have a lot of time to devote to a terrier puppy, you may want to consider an older dog. Puppies require much attention and training while young. They need frequent walks and access to the outside during the housebreaking process. A well trained older dog may be more appropriate for those who cannot be at home during long stretches of time.

Finally, consider the cost of keeping a terrier. Aside from the initial purchase price, an owner must supply routine veterinary care and an adequate, nutritious diet. In addition, many terrier breeds need regular professional grooming. Such costs are considerable and constant throughout the dog's life.

Purchasing Your Terrier

Once you have resolved that a terrier really is the dog for you, you must decide what type you are looking for in order to find the best source for your dog. Which breed is the best fit for your lifestyle? Keep in mind that terriers vary greatly in size, coat (length, shedding, grooming, etc.), and character (aggressive versus more sociable). Are you looking for a show competitor or a companion? If you are looking for a pet, your resources are many. If you are seriously searching for a potential winner in competitive contests, you need to do even more research and make a careful selection.

Selecting a puppy destined to be a show dog is a gamble, as a dog's final physique will not be apparent until the dog is mature. Most puppies are purchased at eight to ten weeks of age—a time when little of the mature physique can be accurately evaluated. Most terriers develop rather slowly, often reaching physical maturity and acquiring their adult coloring at 24 months or later. Selections made prior to this are guesses at best; you can only base your choice upon pedigree and the breeders' knowledge of their dogs. If possible, hold off purchasing a show prospect until it is at least four to six months of age, when a slightly more reliable evaluation can be made. Puppies deemed "show quality" generally demand a hefty purchase price.

There are many outlets for those seeking a dog for a companion. Breeders of show dogs should also be able to supply "pet-quality" dogs. Potential champions are rare, and most litters contain well-bred terriers that are not competitive quality because of some minor fault. Such puppies are often very safe bets, as the pedigrees of both dam (female dog) and sire (male dog) are known and the puppies have been raised during the formative stages by knowledgeable people. The price of such puppies, reflecting their heritage and the care they have been given, will generally range from several hundred dollars up.

Pet terriers can also be purchased from pet stores or neighborhood litters. If you consider a pet-store dog, I suggest that you investigate from where the puppy was purchased and get as much information as possible

Various types of terriers: an Airedale, a Norwich, and a Boston.

Children and terriers can be great companions, but be sure the children know how to properly handle the dog, as this will lead to a safe, healthy relationship for both dog and child.

on its initial care. Many pet shops have been branded as selling inferior, often unhealthy puppies purchased from the "puppy mills" of midwestern America where the animals are mass-produced from whatever breeding stock is at hand. Research should quickly tell you about the pet-store puppy's beginnings. Terriers bought from pet shops are often priced higher than pet-quality dogs available at established kennels, so bear this in mind.

Neighborhood litters are a popular source for pet terriers at a reasonable price. Before you buy you should verify that both the mother and father are registered purebreds and that your puppy's litter is regis-

tered or eligible for registration with the American Kennel Club. Without such confirmation you cannot be assured that you are buying a pure-bred terrier and the price should reflect this. A puppy from a neighborhood litter can, however, still be a fine representative of its breed.

To help in your search, the names and addresses of local and national terrier organizations can be obtained by searching the Internet or writing to the American Kennel Club, 260 Madison Avenue, New York, New York 10016 (*www.akc.org*). Another informative source is the AKC's monthly publication, *American Kennel Club Gazette,* which contains a breed column, a list of advertising kennels, information on all aspects of dog care, and upcoming show and trial listings. *Dog World* and specialty terrier publications are great sources of authoritative information.

What to Look for in a Terrier Puppy

Your terrier puppy should be carefully evaluated for general health and essential breed characteristics. Before you inspect your potential puppy, look closely at the environment in which it was raised. The kennel or living quarters should be neat, clean, and free from parasites. Try to see the litter as a whole. Choosing a good puppy from a poor litter is risky.

Familiarize yourself with the breed standard and use it as a guideline. It is preferable that you see both dam and sire to get a general impression of the size and type of stock from which your puppy stems. In many cases only the dam is available, but she partially indicates whether the litter traces to healthy beginnings. Remember, however, that the dam may appear run-down after the rigors of whelping and nursing a litter. In this case, ask to see a prepregnancy picture. If your puppy's litter is the result of a repeat mating, ask to see some of the maturing dogs from the previous litter or for the name and phone number of an owner. This is especially important when purchasing a show prospect.

In evaluating an eight-week-old puppy, note first its overall appearance. Remember that most of the dog's growth will take place during the first 12 months and that different skeletal areas grow at different rates. A dog at this early stage is apt to appear slightly out of balance. However, a puppy should be clean, pleasant smelling, and plump. Bloating, however, can indicate worm infestation. The eyes should be clear and without discharge and the ears should be pink inside. In several terrier breeds the puppy's coat is not even close to its mature color, so bear this in mind.

The puppy should be full of enthusiasm and should not shy away too easily. To test this, gently remove it from its littermates and see if it still continues to wag its tail or show interest in play. Timidity is not typical of a terrier.

In dog show competition each entry vies to be selected as the dog that best represents the ideal image of the breed as defined by the official standard.

Dogs and cats can learn to live together peacefully if properly introduced and carefully monitored during the first few weeks together.

In addition, you should become acquainted with the genetic disorders that may be present within the breed you desire. If there are inheritable disorders known for the breed, be sure to ask the breeder for certification that the breeding stock was tested and found clear. By doing this, you may spare yourself the heartache of later discovering that your terrier either carries or indeed is inflicted by such devastating disorders as hip dysplasia, elbow dysplasia, patellar luxation, Legg-Calve-Perthes disease, sebaceous adenitis, and congenital deafness, which are associated with some terrier breeds. For a more detailed discussion of terrier disorders, see Chapter 6, "Health Care."

What Age Is Best?

Most puppies are purchased at eight to ten weeks of age, when they are developmentally in what is known as the "human socialization period." This period, which lasts only until the puppy is about three months old, is the best time in a dog's life for it to learn to live with humans.

Experts recommend that a puppy be separated from its dam and littermates and placed in a home during the eighth week of life because it is forming permanent bonds at this time. If allowed to remain with the litter, the primary bond will be to dogs rather than humans, which is a hindrance to the human-dog relationship. Conversely, it is also important that a puppy not be removed from the litter before eight weeks—during

Typical of their breed, these Cairn Terrier puppies are bright, alert, and adorable.

the "canine socialization period"—because this period with dam and littermates is essential to produce a dog that can get along with other animals. Terriers are especially prone to aggressive behavior toward other dogs. If removed from the litter too early, the puppy may not have fully learned the lessons of animal socialization; the result is likely to be an adult dog that reacts too aggressively or too submissively when it meets another dog. Such dogs often become fighters or "fear biters" who are so easily upset that they lash out at other dogs and people. Puppies born in the so-called "puppy mills" are often taken from their litters at six or seven weeks of age so that they can arrive in pet stores at the most adorable age—eight weeks. While this gets the puppies to the market at their most "salable" time,

it can have dire effects on the normal socialization process.

If you cannot arrange to pick up your puppy at approximately eight or nine weeks of age, ask that it begin to have foster human care rather than be left with the litter until you can bring it home.

The Purchase Agreement

Once you have selected your puppy and settled with the breeder on a purchase price, make it official by putting the terms of the deal in writing. This often prevents later difficulty if the dog proves unacceptable for health reasons or if you fail to

When choosing a puppy, try to see the sire and/or dam as well, as this will show you the look of the adult your dog will someday be, as here with these Airedales.

receive all the documents promised you. The breeder should allow the new owner a set number of days to return the puppy if it fails a health examination by the new owner's veterinarian. Get this condition in writing. Such an agreement should also clarify whether an ill dog will be replaced or if the purchase price will be refunded.

At the time of sale, the breeder should supply you with the puppy's American Kennel Club registration application, most of which is filled out by the breeder. This application includes the names and AKC numbers of the sire and dam, information on the puppy's litter, and the name and address of the puppy's new owner. The new owner completes the form by listing two possible names for the puppy, signing, and enclosing the proper fee. If all is in order, the paperwork should take about three to

four weeks to process and you will receive an AKC registration certificate. All forms are also available from the AKC at *www.akc.org*.

If you are buying a puppy from a show-oriented kennel, the breeder may impose some special conditions. In the case of a top-quality animal, the breeder may stipulate terms concerning future matings. (But in most cases a breeder would keep a potential top contender.) With pet-quality puppies from such kennels the breeder may agree to sell the dog only if the new owner agrees not to breed it. In the case of a puppy carrying a disqualifying fault, the breeder may even withhold the puppy's registration papers until proof is supplied that the dog has been neutered. The breeder may offer an attractive selling price to close such a deal. Such dogs can still make fine pets.

Chapter Three

Training Your Terrier

Terriers are a highly energetic, intelligent lot. Left unchecked, these characteristics could lead the dog charging down the wrong behavioral path. Properly channeled, these same traits can help produce a well-mannered, enthusiastic, reliable companion. Most terriers exhibit a lot of spunk, independence, and a zest for life. This must be tempered and guided by a large dose of discipline, right from the start.

When it is quite young, a dog learns its first lessons on manners from its mother. The mother is the undisputed leader and maintains her position by swift discipline whenever a puppy gets out of line. She admonishes her young by using a progression of techniques, starting with low, guttural growls, then (if needed) a swat of the paw, and (if really pushed) a quick shake of the offender's neck. Rarely is any further action required. The mother reacts fairly, unemotionally, and consistently, and the puppies respect her authority. She is the boss—the "alpha figure."

This pattern of discipline traces back to earliest times when dogs roamed in packs. From the pack, one leader emerged; all other pack members then assumed various ranks behind the leader. The leader's authority would occasionally be challenged by the underlings, many of whom competed for independence and power. Even today every dog assumes it is "top dog" until proven otherwise (I call this the "leader of the pack syndrome"). A leader must clearly show any upstart by swift reprimand that its place is not at the head of the pack. Once all pack members submit to the leader's authority, they follow and cooperate fully.

This heritage of pack behavior is still significant today and must be dealt with in your terrier's training. You must take over the leadership position vacated by the puppy's mother by becoming the new alpha figure. Your dog must also be taught to be respectful of all humans, not only the alpha. While this might sound harsh, it really isn't. The owner must simply learn to discipline the dog in a manner it understands and respects. Screaming, brutalizing, whining, or pleading will not make your dog feel compelled to

A well-trained dog, like this Scottie, makes a wonderful companion in the home and outdoors.

respond. A worthy leader does not act that way. Generally all that is needed is a firm vocal reprimand (in a low tone, similar to a dog's warning growl). Hitting and yelling are counterproductive actions that do little except confuse the dog and interfere with the human-dog bond. A leader corrects *every* misdeed immediately, firmly, fairly, and consistently. Letting some misdeeds go uncorrected will undermine a leader's authority.

Basic obedience training is not a spirit-breaking process but rather a confidence-building one. Training teaches the dog the rules of proper behavior in the home, in public, and in the presence of other animals. To get a spirited, sometimes willful terrier to obey commands, the dog must be shown that compliance brings rewards (petting, praise), while disobedience brings disadvantages (scolding and your displeasure). You will find that your terrier loves to please you, adores praise and affection, and does not resent correction or punishment when it is due.

Setting the limits of your dog's actions is your responsibility. The dog must be shown clearly and consistently what is acceptable behavior and what is not. You can't let Rocco share your popcorn and sit on the sofa at night and scold him the next morning for napping there or trying to taste your cheese Danish. You are giving the dog mixed signals. Unvarying and repeated corrections are necessary for your dog to understand your rules and learn to obey. Most behavioral problems arise from poor teachers rather than poor learners. Trainers must be unmistakably clear about what is expected and how things are to be done and must be prepared to show the dog how to react, correct the dog's mistakes, show the procedure again, and praise each little success. Dogs learn by repeated simple patterns of correction and praise, and each dog learns at its own pace.

Training the Terrier Puppy

The first steps to a well-mannered terrier should be taken when the puppy arrives in the new owner's home. Of course, an eight-week-old puppy cannot understand or respond to formal commands, but it can learn that some things please the master and result in a pleasurable experience and some things don't. All training should enforce the idea that learning not only is fun but also brings positive responses from the owner. Learning need not be unpleasant.

Nothing inspires a desire to learn more than success. Make the first training goals simple. An easily accomplished task is to get the dog to respond to its name. Simply use the name whenever dealing with the dog, and offer high praise when it reacts properly. This gives the dog a quick success and the rewards of a proper response. Terriers thrive on positive reinforcement and quickly form a lifelong bond to their masters who treated them lovingly in the early weeks of life.

With each little training success your terrier will gain confidence both in itself and in you. The dog learns that you respond positively when it reacts in a certain manner to certain situations. If it acts otherwise, it is corrected. This consistent praise/correction pattern lays the foundation for learning. Mistakes will be made, but with precise guidelines the dog learns what it may and may not do. Formal training is simply teaching the dog that certain actions or commands require certain reactions.

If you do not want your terrier on your furniture, you must be consistent from the first day your dog comes to your home.

Housetraining

Housetraining is the puppy's first real challenge. If handled properly, training should not be a painful experience for owner or pet. Since terriers take to this task naturally, it should be accomplished rather quickly.

The owner must first understand *when* the puppy will need to eliminate: after eating, after waking, after strenuous play, first thing in the morning, last thing at night. These are definite times. There will also be in-between times. The puppy will usually give cues that indicate the need to eliminate, such as looking uneasy, sniffing, and walking in circles as if searching for something. Until three to six months of age a puppy has very limited control of its

bladder and cannot physically "hold it." Such control will be mastered later.

The key to housetraining success is being an attentive owner: knowing when the puppy will need to eliminate, monitoring its physical signs, getting the puppy out quickly, and praising each little success.

Terriers, like all dogs, retain a pack instinct. One of the pack traits is the desire to keep the "den" area clean. Puppies learn quickly to eliminate away from the sleeping quarters or suffer a motherly correction. By the time your puppy reaches your home, it probably already knows that some areas are acceptable for elimination and others are not. This applies to puppies that were raised by their dams until weaning. The owner must build on this early indoctrination.

Always remember that housetraining is a learning process and mistakes are inevitable. Since most

Housetraining is a learning process, and mistakes will be made, but control will come with time.

"accidents" are not incidents of willful misbehavior, they should be dealt with calmly. Until the puppy truly understands the proper procedure, there should be no punishment for mistakes—just a correction and an indication of what proper behavior is. React in a manner the puppy can understand (that is, react as its dam would). Correct swiftly, firmly, fairly. Show displeasure by sternly saying, "No!" and giving the dog an angry look. Show the dog the proper procedure by taking it to the correct elimination area and lavishly praising it. *Never* hit the puppy or rub its nose in its excrement. Such confusing and humiliating acts are damaging not only to the housetraining process but also to the bond you are trying to establish with your dog.

As your terrier matures, it will gain control of its bodily functions, but until that time, there will be accidents. When you discover an unwanted deposit, *do not overreact.* Let the dog know you are displeased, but you must also let it know exactly what you are displeased about. You must help the dog make a connection between the excrement on the floor and your attitude. Don't assume by your dog's "guilty" behavior that it knows why you are upset. When the dog skulks away to a far corner, tail between legs, it is exhibiting a fear reaction, not a guilty conscience. Immediately remove the dog to the proper elimination area.

Remember, screaming, brutalizing, and carrying on over housetraining mistakes accomplish nothing productive. Such actions confuse and frighten the dog, and will not even reinforce the owner's position as leader.

When you are faced with a cleanup, wash the area with a solution designed to remove excrement odors (available from veterinarians and pet shops) or with a soapy solution containing a little vinegar. Do not use an ammonia-based cleaner, as this will reattract the dog to the spot rather than repel it.

Establish a routine from the first day the puppy is in your house. A very young puppy should be taken out almost hourly during waking hours and given a chance to eliminate. Giving the dog this much attention may seem like a burden, but things get better and it is worth it in the end. Over time, the number of trips outside will be reduced to just a few a day at maturity. Patience is of the utmost importance. A puppy that is rushed and harshly punished during this vital stage of training will often become a chronic soiler as an adult.

A "quick fix" that must be avoided is the tendency to just open the door and let the dog go out by itself. A puppy is easily distracted and may spend its time outside investigating the environment rather than eliminating. Once inside, the puppy may then relieve itself, incurring the wrath of the owner who "just took the dog out." Always accompany the dog during the training period. A puppy needs instruction and, most of all,

Training from an early age is essential, especially for the more assertive terrier breeds, such as this Staffordshire Bull Terrier.

praise. Praise is the most effective training tool the owner has, and it should be used lavishly.

Until the dog is reliably housebroken, limit its access to unsupervised areas of the household. If given the run of the house, it will regard the entire house as its playground. A puppy does not want to soil its den, but it does not regard its playground as highly. Establish an area that will serve as the sleeping quarters and an area for elimination. If possible, have this elimination area outside, rather than a papered area in the house (see "Paper and Litter Box Training," page 26). The intermediate paper stage is necessary only if the owner cannot be present in the

A crate is a valuable aid in the house-training process and provides this West Highland White Terrier puppy with a place to stay when it must be alone. This crate can also be used for safe traveling.

home for long stretches of time during the training process. Bring the puppy to the same elimination spot each time it shows signs of needing to go, and praise *every* success. Correct each mistake firmly but fairly, and immediately return the puppy to the correct spot. Repetition, correction, and praise form the backbone of the housetraining process.

You can help your own cause by following a schedule for feeding the puppy, feeding the prescribed amount (no snacks), and removing the water bowl at night. These easy steps help to regulate the dog's elimination needs and help you predict when the dog will need to go out.

When not under direct supervision, the puppy should be confined to a limited area of the household or crated. Choose a small, uncarpeted area and block off all escape routes. A mesh baby gate will do well for most terrier breeds, but may not be high enough for some of the larger, more nimble breeds, such as the Airedale.

Crates

Crates are effective training tools, and should not be regarded as prisons. Crating a puppy is the most efficient method of housetraining, and is not cruel or inhumane. Most dogs take quite easily to the crate and instinctively try to keep this den area clean by not eliminating in it.

Crates can be purchased from pet shops and dog supply stores. They are most often constructed of heavy-duty plastic or wire mesh. A crate must be large enough for the dog to sit or lie down comfortably.

When used together with a regular schedule of walks and feeding, the crate is a very valuable tool. Of course, it should not be abused. A puppy will be forced to relieve itself if confined for too long a stretch of time. This defeats the purpose of the crate. The owner must take the dog to its proper elimination area at regular intervals and offer enthusiastic approval there each time it relieves itself. Terriers, which thrive on praise, will soon make the connection between eliminating in this area and admiration from their owners. This is the big breakthrough!

A growing puppy has many requirements. It must be fed at least three times a day (7:00 A.M., 12:00 noon, and 5:00 P.M. are common times) and walked very frequently. The puppy can be crated for brief periods between the walks. It is often helpful to remain in the room with the puppy during the first few cratings. Pay no attention to the dog unless there are signs of distress. Terriers are very intuitive. If they sense anxiety in their owner's behavior they may either use this to their advantage (they are quite bright and can be manipulative); on the other hand, they may feel there really *is* something to be feared (since the master is obviously upset) and become unnerved by the crating experience. Many people find this hard to believe, but most dogs enjoy their crates and regard it as a comforting place to rest and relax. While in the crate, the dog will usually sleep.

The first cratings should last only five to ten minutes. This time can be increased gradually over the next few weeks. During the day, puppies under 12 weeks of age may remain in the crate for up to one hour; puppies 12 to 16 weeks of age may be crated for up to two hours; older puppies may stay a maximum of three to four hours in a crate. The maximum time allowed in the crate, which will vary from dog to dog, depends on the dog's age and its elimination requirements. After the initial training period, dogs of all ages can be crated overnight.

The location of the crate is important. It should be placed out of the direct line of household traffic, but not somewhere that will make the dog feel totally isolated. A blanket or towel can be placed on the bottom of the crate for additional comfort, and the dog should be permitted a chew toy or bone. Do not place bowls of food or water in the crate with an unhousebroken puppy.

Once the dog is fully housebroken, the need for the crate is generally gone, but many dogs enjoy having a "den" and will often return to an open crate for naps.

After your terrier is mature enough to be fully housetrained, you can put a small water bowl in the crate if you will be gone for more than a few hours.

Paper and Litter Box Training

Paper training is the slowest method of housetraining, but it is useful for those who cannot be with the puppy for long periods during the day. A puppy cannot be expected to "hold it" all day while its owner is at work. Paper training provides a reasonable alternative until the dog gets older.

Alternatively, some owners of small terriers—especially those who live in urban settings—opt to litter train their dogs. Supplies are available in most pet stores. The downside of this is the expense, the cleanup, and the fact that this may become a lifelong method rather than a stopgap procedure.

Whenever you are not with the puppy, confine it to a limited space. This space should then be divided

Shrinking the size of the papers as the dog progresses, and moving them outside before stopping their use can help the dog "connect" with the outside being the proper location.

into three areas: the elimination area, the feeding area, and the sleeping or crate area. (Many people who paper train also leave the puppy an opened crate to use as a den during the day.) Place several layers of newspapers in the elimination area, making sure that paper does not extend into the other two areas.

Familiarize the puppy with the elimination area by placing the dog on the paper each time you think it needs to eliminate and every time the dog seems agitated. Encourage the puppy with "Do your business," "Good dog on the paper," or some similar phrase that does not include the words "come," "sit," or "down," as these will be used later when basic obedience commands are being taught. Putting a small piece of previously urine-soiled paper on each fresh pile of paper will help to reattract the dog to the elimination spot. Whenever the dog uses the papers, praise it highly to let it know that this area is acceptable for elimination and that you are pleased when it goes there.

Most terriers are real "outdoors" dogs and will readily accept appropriate outside locations when they are mature. Gradually shrink the area covered with newspapers until it is quite small. You might even place some sheets of paper outside a few times to let the dog know that the new elimination spot is acceptable.

At approximately six to twelve months of age most dogs gain enough control to make it through the day. After every "accident-free" extended stay in the house, praise the dog for not soiling and immediately take it to the elimination area. Owners who work outside the home should make sure to walk the dog just before leaving and as soon as returning.

Waste Cleanup

It is up to the owner to clean up after a pet. In many cities the law requires an owner to remove the solid waste excreted by pets, and owners who do not comply face fines ranging from $25 to $250.

Cleaning up such waste not only rids the streets and public areas of offensive and unhealthful materials, but also proves that dog owners as a whole are responsible people. Without such care, apartment dwellers will find it increasingly difficult to find housing where their pets are accepted.

The cleanup process is really quite easy. Scoops made just for this purpose are available in most pet stores. Another method is to invert a plastic bag to cover your hand, pick up the waste using the bag as a shield, allow the waste to fall back into the bottom of the bag, and dispose of it in the nearest garbage container.

Rules for the Trainer

When deciding when to begin formal training, let the puppy be your guide. It is useless and frustrating for

Training should be a fun experience for your dog, with frequent treats for good behavior.

all involved to begin training a puppy that cannot understand what you want of it. As a general rule, most terriers can begin command training at six to eight months of age, but you can instill the desire to learn as young as six or eight weeks of age. Reward each simple success—coming toward you when called, stopping an action when asked—with loads of praise and treats.

Concentration is the key. If the puppy consistently wanders off—physically or mentally—it is probably too young, so try again in a few weeks.

The first lessons should be short, no more than ten minutes, but they

Encouragement and praise are valuable not only in training but also in cementing the bond with your terrier.

should be held regularly—twice daily if possible. Repeat all lessons frequently, but proceed very slowly. Stop as soon as the dog shows signs of having trouble concentrating. Boredom in the early stages can cause serious damage to the dog's acceptance of future training.

Training should be serious, but not tedious. The more fun it is for the dog, the more the dog will benefit from training. Learning can be a stress-producing experience for the dog, so encourage and reassure it frequently. Praise the dog for each minor success, but don't go overboard and get the dog so excited that it forgets what the purpose of the lesson is. Praise enough to inspire the dog to do well and earn more praise.

Commands should be made in an authoritative, but not scolding, tone. Never whine or plead with the dog to get it to comply. Remember: you are the alpha figure! Issue the *same* command each time you request a certain action (not "Rocco, come" one time and "Come here, boy" the next). As a general rule, include the dog's name in any command that requires motion (heel, come) but omit it from the commands where the dog is to remain motionless (sit, down, stay). Similarly, give your terrier cues to what its response to a command will be by always stepping off with your *left* foot when the dog is to move out with you and with your *right* foot when you move away from the dog alone. These are some of the little things that have an unconscious effect on your dog's response.

Owners should understand that terriers are quite *sight sensitive,* and that this affects training. Terriers are instinctively attracted to any sudden movement—from the rustling of leaves to the movements of squirrels. These things alert their senses and awaken instinctive drives to pursue the moving object. Terriers (especially males) are also aggressive toward any dogs they feel are in competition with them. Curbing such impulses is at best difficult. The preferred solution is to minimize the chance of such distractions during the initial stages of training by choosing a location that is distraction-free. The best site for early training is a well-lit, well-ventilated room that is as spacious and uncluttered as possible. Later, once the dog has shown that it has mastered basic techniques, adding distractions such as those found outdoors will test how well your terrier really knows and complies with the commands. If the dog forgets all that it has learned once it is asked to perform in a public spot, retreat to the more secluded training site for more drilling.

Remember, instincts will remain no matter how well a dog is trained. A well-trained dog, however, will be able to control its desires to a great extent. In time, it will perform reliably despite its inborn desire to chase after each unknown rustle in the underbrush. The best indicator of success is slow, steady improvement. This requires patience and encouragement. Work up to more complicated lessons very gradually—and praise, praise, praise!

Gain your terrier's attention before starting any lesson. Get the dog to make eye contact with you. This is the first step in inspiring interest, since an encouraging look from you creates in the dog anticipation and a desire to please.

Patience and consistency are the keys to effective training. Progress very slowly, as any action quickly learned is often quickly forgotten. Many repetitions of every action will be needed before the dog will really know how it is expected to respond. Give and enforce each command in the exact same way each time. The dog must then perform the required response fully—in the same way each time. Such drilling can test anyone's patience, but the repetitions eliminate confusion.

Verbal corrections are an instantaneous, "No!" You must then repeat the command and show the proper response once again. Repeat the command only when absolutely necessary; your goal is to have the dog perform the action when given only one command.

Correct fairly and with love, not out of anger. The dog is probably making mistakes out of confusion, not willful misbehavior. Never shout at or strike the dog. This will only make matters worse and possibly ruin the dog for further training. Since your terrier's enthusiasm is a great asset, you do not want to break its spirit. Emphasize the dog's successes rather than harp on its mistakes.

The severity of your correction must depend on the cause of your terrier's failure. Reprimanding a confused dog will be ineffective and in the long run will undermine the training process. Monitor the dog's body language for signs of distress or confusion (often reflected in a sunken posture and flatly drawn back ears). If confusion is evident, encourage your dog to succeed by breaking down the task into its sim-

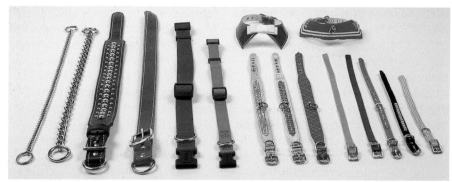

Collars come in a great variety of sizes and styles, so be sure to pick one that is appropriate for your terrier's size and strength.

plest elements, leaving no chance of error. Praise, admire, celebrate! Taking such care should improve your terrier's chances of becoming a reliably trained pet, rather than a discouraged or disgruntled misfit.

Keep the lessons short and pleasant. If you quit while your dog is encouraged by its success and still eager, it will remain interested in learning more. Don't get carried away and push your terrier beyond its capabilities when things are going well. Continually asking the dog for "just one more" can lead to exhaustion and disinterest. If things aren't going well, don't give in to anger or frustration. Instead, revert to some simple action that the dog *can* succeed in, offer congratulations, and call it a day. Things will probably go more smoothly the next time.

Follow each lesson with a generous dose of approval and a pleasant activity, such as a walk or a game. Your terrier will appreciate the special attention and think of the training process as pleasurable.

Breaking to Collar and Leash

The collar and leash (or lead) are the primary tools of training. When formal training is to begin, you will need to purchase a training or "choke" collar, which consists of a chain of metal links with a ring on each end. The training collar allows you to apply as much pressure as necessary to evoke the correct response by the dog. A light snap upwards is all that is needed to get the dog's attention and persuade it to correct its misdeed. The collar will momentarily tighten. Once the pressure is released, the collar will immediately loosen. Your dog will quickly learn that the upward tug and the resulting tightening signify your displeasure and that a correction is needed. Used properly, the training collar is a valuable teaching aid. It should *never* be used inhumanely to inflict pain.

Choose a collar that is the appropriate size for your terrier—approxi-

This American Staffordshire puppy naturally wants to chew on its new lead, but the owner should gently tug on it and tell the dog "No!"

mately the diameter of the head plus one or two inches. Overly large collars can be dangerous and are useless for quick corrections, so don't buy one the puppy will "grow into."

The training collar is to be worn *only* during lessons. Between lessons a lightweight nylon or leather collar can be worn continuously. Attach a medallion to this type of collar on which the dog's name, your name, address, and phone number are listed. Any medical problems the dog may have should be inscribed as well. This tag can be invaluable should your terrier wander too far in search of a scent and become lost, or if it is involved in an accident.

Once you have placed a collar on the dog, offer praise and let the dog wear it for a while to familiarize itself with the new weight. When the dog no longer balks at the feel of the collar, attach the training leash which is generally made of a light but sturdy webbed cloth, nylon, or leather. Correct with "No!" if the dog tries to chew the lead. If necessary, apply a slight upward tug to remove it from the dog's grasp. The leash is a symbol of authority, not a toy, so be firm. At first you can let the puppy drag the lead around to accustom it to this sudden weight, but closely monitor the dog's movement to make sure it does not get tangled or hurt. A three-foot leash is best for training pur-

poses, as it does not allow the dog to lag behind or forge too far ahead.

The next step is to pick the lead up, but apply no pressure. Follow the puppy around for several minutes, and then let the pup know that it is time to follow you. Slowly introduce the feel of the upward tug. If the dog is frightened, reassure it, but

An identification tag firmly attached to the collar is an important aid to retrieving a lost pet.

rier), you may have to modify some of the basic training techniques to compensate for the extreme difference in height between you and your dog. A solid lead will aid the task. This is basically a rod with a short expanse of leash at its end. Held near your side it allows you to keep your pet in proper position without having to hunch over or clutch the several feet of leash that would otherwise extend above the dog's head.

The solid lead is held in your right hand. In your left hand hold a back scratcher or a similar aid with which you can reach down and position the dog. With this method you do not need to bend continuously to correct the dog. You can even use the back scratcher to scratch the dog's back gently as a form of praise.

Training small dogs can be complicated (and backbreaking). If your pet fails to progress, seek the guidance of a trainer who can demonstrate some of the more effective techniques for handling small terriers. Through experimentation you should be able to work out a method that is effective and comfortable for both you and your dog.

Remember, small or toy terriers are not to be treated as fragile objects; they, too, need manners. Reinforce this concept from an early

continue to apply firm pressure whenever it wanders out of your control area. In a short time you should be able to impress on the puppy that the lead is a restraint that must be obeyed and that the gentle tugs demand immediate attention. Your terrier will soon be walking according to your guidance. At this point, more formal instruction can begin.

Tips for Training Small or Toy Terriers

When training some of the smaller terriers, particularly the toy breeds (such as the Yorkshire or Silky Terage: do not carry them all the time and do not pamper them. They will need additional consideration, of course, and some added encouragement. In the initial stages of training you could teach the dog the fundamental commands by having it stand at your side on a sturdy crate or other elevated surface. Once the dog is aware of what you want, start the process over again with the dog positioned at your feet. Most dogs make the transition very smoothly.

Encourage the dog to look up frequently, as eye contact is a vital part of a training program. You can accomplish this by making a short, staccato sound to get the dog's attention. If this fails, or if you feel silly making clucking noises (who could blame you?), you can gently tap the top of the dog's head with the training back scratcher or dangle a tempting tidbit or favorite toy in the air. Use your imagination and devise a system that works for you. The important point is that by making eye contact you are encouraging the dog to pay attention. Without the dog's attention, little progress will be made. After a few weeks, as the dog's familiarity and interest in the training process increases, you can stop the attention-getting maneuvers.

Clicker Training

When beginning your training program, you should consider a relatively new method of training called clicker training. It is based on posi-tive reinforcement and works well with many terriers. Rewards and treats are great training aids. Some dogs need little more than an occasional piece of kibble and a pat, while others react most favorably to audible stimulus. These dogs do well with clicker training, which is touted as the most gentle form of training, as there is no reliance on leash or collar and the resultant tugs.

Clicker training has been adapted from the work of psychologist B. F. Skinner, who posited that behavior can be shaped without force. Dogs can be taught to perform a behavior consistently and happily in return for praise and the occasional treat. The clicker becomes a reinforcer that the dog associates with fun, food, and affection.

Clickers are low-tech wonders. They can be purchased in a five-pack for around $10. At this price, they can be spread around the house, yard, and car. The first step is to make a connection in the dog's mind between the behavior, the clicker, and getting a treat. The key to success with this method, and all others, is patience. Training a dog in this manner avoids the pitfall of having an animal that responds compulsively rather than willingly. As training progresses, the treats are often unnecessary, as the sound of the clicker is like hearing "Good girl!"

For example, the "sit" is taught at first without even using a command or placing hands on the dog. Every time the dog goes into the sit position, sound the clicker and give a treat. Once the dog connects that sitting is rewarded, the command "sit" is added directly before the click is given. As the dog progresses, the clicks are always given but the treats become random.

Clicker training is often tougher for the owner to learn than the dog. Anyone who has trained dogs the "traditional" way may need to take a course from a trainer experienced in this method, as old habits are hard to break. Many longtime dog fanciers have found clicker training to be a more successful and rewarding method for dealing with terriers, who can show a stubborn streak. At best, clicker training can be used in combination with other training methods, making learning a fun process for all.

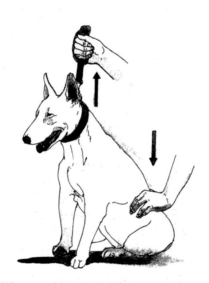

When teaching the "sit," apply upward pressure on the leash while pressing down on the hindquarters.

The Basic Commands

While only a dedicated few terriers and trainers are destined for high honors in the obedience trial rings, to be a trustworthy companion *every* terrier must master some basic commands. Two that are rather easily taught and learned are "no" and "off," which are more corrections than commands. The five basic commands that require more formal instruction are: "sit," "stay," "heel," "come," and "down." Upon learning to respond to these commands, your terrier will have earned a place in human company. Lacking this knowledge, the dog lacks restraint and should be kept on leash, tethered, or otherwise restricted from activities that require self-control and manners.

Sit

The "sit" is taught with the dog on leash, preferably indoors in a quiet location. At first the dog should be taught to sit at your left side, with its shoulders square to your leg. Later, once it has mastered this position, it can be taught to sit in front of you. Begin by placing the dog at your left side, while you hold the leash taut in your right hand, applying only enough upward pressure to keep the dog's head up. Command "Sit" while you firmly press your left hand on its rear to place it in the sitting position. Continue the upward pressure from the lead in your right hand and use the left to straighten your pet's position. Praise your dog as soon as it is properly positioned and release with "Good dog!" or an upward sweep of the left hand.

Make the first few attempts quite short, thus not allowing the dog the opportunity to fall over on your leg or lie down. Gradually increase the required sitting time and be sure to praise the dog when it reaches the sit position—not as it breaks to get up. It must learn to associate the praise with the completion of the action. Should the dog attempt to move out of position, correct with "No!" and a slight jerk of the lead.

As the dog progresses, the amount of pressure you apply on the rear should be reduced and finally removed. Within a short time the sitting action will become habitual in response to the command. Once you reach this point you can begin training the "stay" and the "heel."

Stay

The "stay" command builds from the "sit." Do not attempt to teach the "stay" until your dog is reliably performing the "sit," as the dog will be required to remain in "sit" position until released.

Begin by placing the dog in a "sit." Keep some slight upward pressure on its neck from the leash in your right hand. As you command "Stay!" you must simultaneously move away from the dog using your *right* foot and bring the palm of your left hand down toward its face, stopping short of touching its muzzle. Move only a short distance (about a

The "stay" is taught with the dog in the sit position. Move away from the dog as you command "Stay!" and signal with your palm toward the dog.

foot at first) or the dog will try to follow you. Make sure that the hand signal is given at the same time that the command is given and the step taken. Retain eye contact, if possible. Repeat the command while maintaining the signal. The voice should be firm and authoritative. Do not expect the dog to stay for more than ten seconds or so at first; release your pet after small successes and offer praise.

When the dog breaks the "stay," return it immediately to the "sit" and repeat the whole procedure. Never let it get up by its own initiative without a swift correction, as the "stay" is a command that really tests a leader's authority. It is normal but unacceptable for the dog to try to move toward you once it sees you move away, or to lie down once it sees that it is to remain where positioned. Be patient, correct each error, and do not expect immediate results. As you see improvement, extend the length of the time for the "stay" and the distance moved. The desired achievement is a dog that can be relied upon to remain in the "sit" position for at least several minutes. (The "down-stay," to be taught later, can and should be used daily as a more extended control measure.) This procedure requires the dog to maintain a lying down position for 30 minutes or more as a means of teaching the importance of discipline and enforcing your position as leader. It sounds impossible—and perhaps even cruel—but it really is a good method for taming a little of the terrier spunk.

Heel

Most terriers will instinctively bolt forward when given the opportunity to investigate new or even familiar

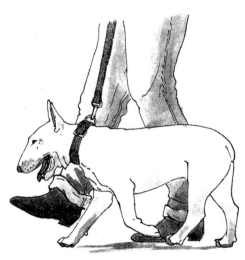

Every terrier should be taught to heel at its master's side when out for a walk.

terrain. To train your dog to walk with you, at your pace, it will need to be taught to "heel." Heeling is no more than controlled walking—an act every dog should be expected to perform. The dog should always be on your left side, its chest preferably in line with your leg. The leash is held in your right hand and corrective pressure is applied by your left. Place the dog in a "sit" and begin by stepping off with your *left* foot, calling "Rocco, heel!" as you move forward. Snap the leash as you give the command to start him forward, removing the pressure as he walks in "heel" position. Walk at a comfortable pace, applying pressure only if he surges ahead or lags behind. Make your snaps firm and repeat "heel!" with each correction. Praise as soon as he responds, using a pleasant tone and "Good dog!" Periodically repeat the praise—but don't overdo it—if the dog remains in proper position for extended lengths of time. As soon as you come to a halt, the dog is to sit. At first you will need to issue the "sit" command, and perhaps help the dog down, but as the dog progresses, the "sit" will become automatic when you stop, and no verbal cue will be needed.

Mastering the "heel" will take time. As you encounter problems—such as your terrier's desire to surge ahead—you may want to resort to placing the dog in a "sit" to restore calm rather than continually snapping it back into proper position. Having the dog sit will allow it to succeed at a task with which it is already familiar, and thereby receive praise. This will keep you both at ease; the heeling practice can then continue rather than break down into confusion on the pet's part and anger on the trainer's. Once the dog has successfully completed the "sit," move it out again with "Rocco, heel!" Offer praise if he comes and moves in the proper position. Stop him as soon as he misbehaves, giving a firm tug on the lead and a stern look.

It is imperative that you do not apply continuous pressure to the neck of a surging dog. The choke collar is effective as a sudden jarring that regains the dog's attention and brings about a correction. The snap on the lead must be swift and strong enough to get a response, but not so strong as to cause pain and possible injury. The choke should be used only when needed, should have an impact on the dog, and should be immediately released.

During the early attempts at heeling, keep the lessons short—no more than 10 to 15 minutes. As the dog becomes more adept—and no longer needs to be put in frequent corrective "sits"—extend the lessons as energy and interest (both yours and the dog's) may indicate. Even a well-trained terrier may react instinctively when it spots a small animal in the brush. Your patience will help your pet master self-restraint. So bear in mind that instinctive drives will often surface and deal with them as simple mistakes, not willful misbehavior.

Come

The "come" teaches a dog that it must return to its master at once, without hesitation. It is a command that will enforce your leadership position, as the dog must learn to stop whatever it is doing and return on command to its master's side. As terriers have a strong interest in whatever they happen to be doing, they are often reluctant to break their concentration to respond to the command. While they may quickly comprehend what the command means and what is expected, getting a reliable, wholehearted response will take time. Accept no less than a quick response every time, or the dog may choose not to obey at a crucial moment. The "come" command can be life-saving when used to remove the dog from danger.

You have already given your terrier informal training in this command. As a pup, it quickly learned to respond happily when called—probably in anticipation of play or food. Now the goal is to have your dog respond to your call regardless of the circumstances or how it perceives the situation (thereby overcoming the "what's in it for me?" syndrome).

Formal training for the "come" command should begin with a pleasant play period. Place the dog on a long leash (20 feet or more) and let it romp in the practice area. Maintain only minimal tension on the end of the lead. Once the dog is relaxed and concentrating on play or investigation of some nearby object, command "Rocco, come!" in a firm

In advanced agility competition, the dog must run a series of obstacles on the course, including an A-frame, jumps of various heights and types, a collapsible tunnel, a dog walk and teeter, and a set of weave poles. The dog and handler team is competing against time.

tone and snap the lead to start the dog in motion toward you. Offer praise as the dog *begins* to move toward you. Have him come directly to you and into a "sit." Should he fail to respond, give a sharp correction with the lead as you repeat "Come!" If necessary, repeat the command. You might have to reel the dog in by slowly retracting the cord—but this is rarely required. Once the dog has completed the "come" and the companion command of "sit," release with "Good dog!" and let him move away from you again. Repeat the "come" command at various intervals. Should the dog fail to move immediately toward you, correct with a sharp snap on the lead.

Use of the "come" should not be overdone. Perform a few repetitions during all training lessons. Employ it also throughout the day when the dog's presence really is requested. *Never* command a dog to come and then punish it for an offense once it arrives at your side. It will associate coming with punishment. If you catch your dog in an inappropriate action, *go to it* and reprimand. If you call the dog and punish it when it arrives, you will almost certainly ruin your chances of having a dog that will instantly return to the "come."

Down

The "down" command is tied closely to the "sit" and "stay" com-

mands. To teach the dog to lie down, place it first in a "sit" and kneel next to it. As you command "Down!" take hold of its front legs near the body, gently lift them from the floor, and lower the dog to the ground. Once down, command the dog to "Down, stay!" Follow this with "Good dog!" if it remains in the prone position. You may need to keep your left hand resting on its back to keep it from getting up. Pet your terrier briefly, release by motioning upward with your hand and gently tugging the lead, and return the dog to a "sit," on command, to begin again.

Do not make your dog remain in the down position too long at first, as the "down" concept needs to be reinforced to keep it clearly differentiated from the stay. Be sure the dog remains lying on all fours for the short downs, not sprawled out on its side. The dog is to be alert on the down, not overly comfortable.

Practice the "down" several times each day. As the downward movement becomes more familiar, you will soon be able to stop guiding the legs down, so you can avoid kneeling down. During this transition you may want to issue the command and try just slapping the floor with the palm of your hand to get the dog moving down. Alternatively, you can place the taut leash under your left foot. As you command "Down!" apply a slight amount of pressure on the dog's shoulders. This should be sufficient to give it the idea.

As the dog progresses, you can teach it to lie down on leash from various positions, such as in front of you, from a distance, etc. You may want to incorporate a down motion with your hand in time with the "down" command. When practicing indoors, you should occasionally have the dog work off leash, but do not accept sloppy performance, as many dogs tend to be less businesslike once the lead is removed. The dog should never be allowed off leash outdoors, unless in a confined area, until it has proven itself truly trustworthy. Even then, any sudden sight or sound could distract even a well-trained terrier and cause it to bolt, so always be on your guard when the dog is off leash.

One of the most valuable commands is the "down-stay. "You should train your dog to perform an extended "down-stay" daily. With practice, you will be able to have your dog remain in a "down-stay" for 30 minutes or more. Not only will this command reinforce your authority in the dog's mind, but it will also give you the control you need to effectively remove the dog from an undesirable activity (such as begging at your dinner table or creating a scene when company comes to the door) without having to lock up the dog. This is not punishment, but rather a lesson in self control. A properly trained dog can be placed in an extended down-stay near its owner, yet in a place where it can relax too, such as across the room or in a corner.

Begin with stays of a few minutes and then gradually increase with stays of nonuniform duration—eight minutes, then five minutes the next time, fifteen minutes the next. In this way the dog will not anticipate when it will be finished and will truly learn to obey the command. Should the dog become bored and start to break the stay, tell it "No, stay!" and replace it. *You* must determine when the dog may rejoin you. As the dog becomes accustomed to the long "down," it will often fall asleep. This is perfectly acceptable as long as it remains where it was placed when it awakens. You should, however, wake the dog with a tap of your foot near its head when it is time to release it (try not to startle it). Do not let it sleep on after the exercise is ended; you must formally complete each exercise. Always end the long "down-stay" with the upward release motion and praise.

The "down" can also be an effective lifesaving command to immediately stop your terrier from participating in a dangerous situation. Once you are certain that the dog understands the "down" concept, the "down" can be practiced while walking, not just from the "sit."

Teaching a dog to drop down on command while in motion takes time, but is well worth the effort. For example, your well-trained terrier has been let out in the backyard; it spots a squirrel and bolts after it, ending up across the road. Upon seeing you, it abandons the chase and immediately begins to run toward you and into oncoming traffic. *Before* the dog reaches the road, you command "Down!" and the dog immediately drops to the ground to safety. Such a case is the extreme, but it emphasizes not only the importance of the "down" command but also the fact that only an immediate response to a command is acceptable.

Chapter Four

Keeping and Caring for Your Terrier

While leaving the security of its dam and littermates can be upsetting for a puppy, most terriers make the transition with great ease. With few exceptions, terriers are very people-oriented and they adapt well to the "human pack." Many become intensely loyal and protective of their masters.

A New Puppy in the Home

An owner can ease the transition by preparing ahead for the new puppy's arrival. Basic supplies to have on hand are: water and food bowls, food designed specifically for a puppy (preferably the food it has already been eating), a bed or crate, puppy-size collar and leash, grooming tools particular to your chosen terrier breed, and some safe chew toys.

The Earliest Lessons

The first few days in your home are an extremely important time, dur-ing which the dog will absorb a lot of information not only about its new territory but also about how you feel about the newcomer. A conscientious owner wants only positive experiences to get imprinted in the dog's mind and strives to make these early days as stress-free as possible.

The puppy's first few weeks in a new home should be devoted to mastering the lessons of living among humans. The dog will learn that there are pros and cons. The pros are the fun and the affection; the cons are the corrections. A puppy certainly can understand some simple lessons and corrections. A puppy's dam has already shown it that there are rules and limits on behavior. A considerable amount of learning takes place while the puppy is quite young, and these lessons are permanently remembered. At this point, the puppy should not have developed any bad habits, so this is a good time to begin teaching basic manners. Through careful monitoring and positive corrections an owner can constructively shape the behavior of the future adult terrier.

These Norwich Terrier puppies enjoy their time outside, but they must be closely watched to be sure they remain safe from falling and injuring themselves.

The First Day

It is best to pick up the puppy from its breeder when you have several vacation days or a long weekend to familiarize the dog with its new home. It would be unfortunate to pick up a puppy one day and leave it alone the next while you go off to work or school; the puppy may feel abandoned and then have great difficulty feeling secure in its new home.

Be sure to treat the puppy gently and to speak to it in soft tones. Even though terrier puppies are pretty rough-and-tumble, roughhousing is not appropriate in the first few days in a new home. Play should be calm and filled with lots of affection and praise. The dog will need to be reassured, comforted, and encouraged during this trying period. Immediately

upon arrival in the home show the newcomer where its food and water bowls are located, as well as the elimination area. Once it has received the basic tour, let the dog roam and explore its new environment on its own, while you, of course, supervise from a distance. Allow the puppy to set the pace, and remember that frequent rest periods are necessary. Reward all good behavior lavishly, with treats and praise.

It will need its own sleeping area, preferably a sleeping box or crate (see more on crates in "Housetraining," page 24). The puppy will return to this "den" for all sleeping periods. Allow the puppy to sniff and investigate this area soon after arriving in the home and return the dog to this sleeping area whenever it shows signs of tiring. Having a place of its own will instill in the puppy a sense of belonging and security during a very upsetting time. Until reliably housetrained, a puppy should be confined whenever it is not being directly supervised.

During the first few days try not to overstimulate the puppy. One way to go easy on the dog is to introduce only the members of the immediate family; save the neighbors for a few days later.

If there are other pets in the home, if possible hold off on letting them meet until the puppy has had a little time to get its bearings. When they meet, make sure all participants are strictly supervised. Praise the animals highly if they remain peaceable toward each other. If any of the animals react negatively, correct improper behavior with a stern warning and remove offenders from the area. Try again at regular intervals. A new puppy is often seen as a rival by established household pets, but this usually eases up as each animal takes its place in the pecking order that animals establish for themselves. Adult male terriers are often quite aggressive toward other dogs, especially other adult males, but they usually react less aggressively toward puppies. Things usually get better with time.

When introducing a terrier to a cat, remember that these two species do not share a common body language and they will probably not react favorably. This is especially true if either or both of the animals is an adult. If a dog has been raised since a puppy with cats, it will generally be peaceable toward cats throughout its life. If, however, an adult terrier is suddenly asked to tolerate a cat, you are asking for trouble.

It is inadvisable to keep as household pets any of the small animals that are the natural prey of terriers. This includes hamsters, mice, guinea pigs, and even rabbits. Should they get out of their cages, most terriers would instinctively go after them aggressively and destroy them. Even the best trained terrier cannot be relied upon to go against its instinct to kill rodents and small predators.

Owners should take pains to avoid jealousy and resentment by showing equal amounts of affection toward all pets in the home. It is easy to get caught up in making the new puppy feel at home, while the old-timers are neglected. This makes for hard feelings.

The First Night

Most puppies will whimper or cry during the first few nights and during periods of short separation. It is important to remember that the experience of the first few nights will shape the course of the nights to come, so do not be too soft-hearted and allow the puppy to sleep with you unless you plan on allowing this in the future. Consistency is at the heart of all training, and you cannot allow the puppy to do something this week that is forbidden the next. The new puppy is justifiably upset and you should do your best to comfort it. Place the dog in its sleeping area, pet it, talk soothingly, and then retire. If the puppy carries on desperately, return to it and comfort it again, but do not stay too long. Do not remove it from the sleeping area or pick it up, as this is reinforcement to the dog that if it howls long enough you will come and get it. You may want to help ease its tension by playing some soft, soothing music or by placing a hot water bottle under its blanket to imitate the mother's warmth. These measures should relieve the dog enough for it to fall asleep. The amount of attention needed should decline each night as the puppy gets used to the process.

Daytime Care

A puppy requires almost constant attention and should not be expected to stay by itself for more than short periods before it is physically mature enough and adjusted to its role in the household. A puppy that is left alone for great lengths of time will feel abandoned. This insecurity will adversely affect the way it bonds with its master, in particular, and possibly with all humans. A lonely puppy often becomes a maladjusted adult dog, and little can be done later to counteract a poor beginning. The result is often a high-strung dog with undesirable habits, such as tension chewing or scratching.

If you must go out for an extended length of time, take the dog with you. If this is impossible, try to leave the dog with someone (preferably someone it is acquainted with). Failing all else, arrange to have someone come to your home several times a day to socialize the puppy and attend to its exercise and elimination needs. Many school-age children will jump at the chance for such a fun part-time job. In many cities, there are professional "dog walkers" that can be hired to watch your dog during this critical period.

These extraordinary measures are important when a puppy or newly acquired dog is not mature enough to handle the physical and emotional stress of an extended separation. Things will improve, however, and early care and nurturing will go a long way to produce a happy, confident terrier adult.

A pet door provides an easy way to give your terrier access to both the house and its fenced-in area outside.

These Bull Terrier puppies will reach their full potential if given plenty of exercise, proper nutrition, and regular training and medical care.

Socialization

Local breed and obedience clubs often sponsor puppy socialization classes in which puppies are taught simple positive behaviors, such as how to walk on a leash, sit, or come. (See also pages 30–40.) These classes are not designed for formal obedience training, but rather as a nonstressful introduction to basic discipline and training techniques.

Such courses are aimed as much on teaching proper methods to the owner as they are focused on the puppy. For a modest fee, instructors outline basic discipline and house-training techniques, explain health and nutrition requirements, and clarify how a puppy learns and understands. This knowledge will enable the owner to establish a position of leadership and gain control over the puppy right from the start. Many novice owners do not understand that a dog expects a leader to behave in certain ways. If the dog does not receive the cues it expects from a leader, it will try to assume that position itself. Puppy socialization classes help produce more effective owners.

The puppy benefits greatly from these socialization classes, as it learns not only vital lessons on life but is exposed to other people and dogs. By having some puppy-to-puppy socialization at an early age, the dog learns how to handle itself when around other animals. Terriers are, by instinct, slightly antagonistic when encountering another dog.

Proper feeding requires more than just filling up a bowl and letting the dog eat until full. There are health consequences that must be considered—especially overfeeding and obesity.

Early socialization is vital to keeping this tendency under control, as the dog will need self-restraint when it meets other animals on the street or in the veterinarian's office. Having a game nature is no excuse for unruly behavior.

This early indoctrination will also instill a sense of accomplishment and self-confidence in the dog, as well as a positive attitude toward training. Puppy socialization classes are highly recommended for owners of terriers.

Feeding

The selection of your dog's daily food is a decision that should not be taken lightly. It will have a direct impact on the dog's overall health and longevity. The primary concern is to select food that is nutritionally complete and balanced.

The main types of dog food are dry, canned, and supplementary. No one type alone is completely satisfactory; most owners find a blend of several to be the best solution.

Dry Food

Dry food is the most commonly used type of dog food, and also the type most likely to vary in quality. Dry foods are generally composed of 8 to 10 percent water; the remaining ingredients are cereals, soy, meat by-products, and small amounts of fats, vitamins, and minerals. Ounce for ounce this is the least expensive type of dog food, and in the long run it may be the most healthful.

The most popular "name" brands are nutritionally complete products; look for the list of nutritional values on the package. There may be great variation, however, in the amount of dry food that must be consumed to fulfill the basic dietary requirements. With some dry products, an excessive amount must be eaten to fulfill your dog's needs. This can be determined by reading the suggested feeding amounts per weight of dog as listed on the package. If large amounts must be ingested, there will be an inevitable increase in waste materials to be excreted. Also, content may vary from batch to batch in many dry food products, as fluctuations in the availability of the base crop (soy, com, barley, etc.) produce a slightly different blending at various times during the year.

The meat-and-meal based dry foods commonly sold in pet stores offer a stable mixture from batch to batch. These dry food brands are nutritionally complete, easily digested, and formulated with enough fiber to help produce a firm stool. Although these products may cost a little more per pound, in the long run they may be less expensive, as the dog does not need to eat as much of it.

One drawback of dry food products is that they tend to be low in fat. This is easily handled by adding approximately half a container of canned food to the dry food as a supplement.

Canned Food

Canned dog foods contain approximately 75 percent water, and the remaining 25 percent is generally meat by-products, soy fillers, vitamins, minerals, artificial coloring, and preservatives. The high water level and additives can have a diuretic effect on many dogs, and this can result in housebreaking problems.

Some canned foods are more nutritious than others, with the ones designed for the various stages of life most recommended. Even these should not comprise the entire diet, but should form no more than one quarter of the daily intake. Canned food should be combined with a high-quality dry food for best results. Most dogs are very fond of canned food, so this is also recommended for dogs needing to gain some weight. Alternatively, this should be limited in overweight dogs.

Supplements

Unlike humans, dogs are not easily bored by a satisfactory diet and can eat the same food every day. However, giving your dog an occasional treat or nutritious snack will do no harm. Since commercially prepared diets can be lacking in roughage, this aspect of the diet can be improved by giving your dog a daily raw carrot, apple, or crunchy biscuit.

Table scraps can result in a case of loose bowels. Small snacks of fruits, vegetables, and cereals will not upset the intestinal tract and may, in fact, help promote proper digestion. The trick is to get the dog trained to enjoy these snacks while still a puppy.

Aside from nursing mothers, most dogs will be able to fulfill all their dietary needs through commercially prepared dog food and will seldom need vitamin supplements. Problems caused by excessive vitamin supplementation are more common than ones from vitamin deficiencies from commercially prepared foods. It is especially important not to oversupplement the diet of growing puppies, as there can be serious side effects. A well-balanced diet, supported by adequate exercise, should be all your dog needs to keep in good trim and good health.

The Feeding Process

Not only is *what* you feed your dog of utmost importance, you must also form a pattern for *where, when,* and *how* you feed your dog. These may seem like lesser concerns, but they help establish a healthy routine.

Your terrier should be allowed adequate time and space to eat its meal in an out-of-the-way place. In the bustle of the kitchen at a busy time of day the dog may be anxious that its food is in danger of being taken away and may develop bad habits in response. One common reaction is to quickly devour the food. Such a habit can lead to digestive problems or a pattern whereby the dog eats too quickly, vomits back the food, and eats it once again. Eating in a high-traffic area also can make the dog over-protective of its food, which certainly is to be avoided. A dog must be trained from an early age to allow its master to pick up and remove the food, if necessary, without the dog's growling or protesting.

When to feed your dog depends mostly on the age of the dog. Young puppies will require four or five small meals a day. This can be reduced to three daily meals at approximately four to six months, with a further reduction to two daily meals at approximately nine months of age. The usual adult dog feeding schedule is either one large meal a day, generally in the late afternoon or at night, or two smaller meals daily.

There can be no set scale for how much food one dog will need daily. An active, hard-working terrier will require more calories per day than an older, slow-moving one. Growing puppies and pregnant or lactating bitches will need a diet high in protein and calories.

To promote healthy eating patterns, keep the feeding process simple. Give the dog some privacy and ample time to eat its meal—generally 15 to 20 minutes. After this time, pick up and discard any leftover food. At the next meal reduce the amount slightly if the dog has been leaving food uneaten. If the bowl is quickly cleared, you may need to increase the amount slightly.

If the dog refuses its food, pick it up and discard it. Do not offer a replacement until the next scheduled meal. Catering to a picky eater will only enhance the problem. How-

Several types of food and water dishes are available. All are sturdy; some include food and water dishes in the same stand.

With proper nutrition, these Airedales will grow to be between 45 and 60 pounds (20.4–27.2 kg) and 23 inches (58.4 cm) tall.

ever, a sudden distaste for eating is generally an indication of either a health or a behavioral problem. The food is probably fine. If the problem persists, have the dog examined by a veterinarian.

A few additional feeding rules are:

• Have an ample supply of clean, fresh water available at all times. This is especially important in hot weather.

• Clean all food and water bowls daily in hot, soapy water and rinse well to inhibit the growth of bacteria.

• Do not make sudden changes in the diet. To avoid digestive upset, introduce new foods slowly, in modest amounts.

• Always bring a supply of the dog's usual food when traveling or when the dog must be kenneled.

• Serve the food at room temperature, not cold from the refrigerator.

Teething and Chewing

While terriers are not noted as compulsive chewers, *all dogs will chew.* It is a natural process, and owners should be aware of it. A puppy will chew to help cut its first teeth, to exercise and strengthen its jaw, and to rid itself of the first teeth. A puppy may do a lot of chewing between four and nine months of age. But don't be fooled into thinking it will all end in a few months. The need to chew will remain as the dog matures.

A dog will need to rid itself of accumulated tartar on the teeth, and

A soft bed and chew toys make this Parson Russell Terrier a happy dog.

the best method for this is through chewing hard substances. Some dogs also use chewing as a method to release tension, often causing extensive and expensive damage to household goods.

Give the dog an ample supply of suitable chew objects and let the dog know what *may* and *may not* be chewed. Do not give the dog an old slipper to chew and then expect it to leave your best oxfords alone.

Rawhide bones are favorites with most dogs, but these can prove to be quite expensive as many dogs can devour them in short order. Nylon bones are long-lasting, safe alternatives, but many dogs find them unappealing. Hard veal bones, such as from the knuckle, should be given sparingly, as they can be constipating as well as too abrasive to the tooth enamel if the dog is a prodigious chewer. Many dogs enjoy chewing on hard rubber balls that are large enough to mouth but not swallow.

During the initial teething stages, confine the dog when it cannot be supervised and give it a suitable chew toy. A crate is best for this (more on crates on page 24).

Chewing can be destructive not only to your household goods, it can also be fatal for the dog. Electric cords are appealing to the inquisitive puppy and can be deadly if plugged in. Some plants are poisonous if ingested (see "Poisonings," page 86), and many dogs are attracted to them by their smell or appearance. If you have poisonous plants, be sure they are inaccessible to the dog.

Obesity

Terriers that are overfed and underexercised are subject to obesity. This is an unnatural state for a terrier, which should be highly active, alert, and ready for any adventure that comes its way.

Obesity is reaching epidemic proportions, not only in humans but also in dogs. It is estimated that nearly 30 percent of pet dogs are overweight. This dramatically increases the dog's chances of heart and liver disease, joint inflammation and arthritis, skeletal problems, heat intolerance, metabolic and respiratory diseases (such as diabetes), and lowered resistance to disease.

A "rib test" will help you determine if your terrier's body fat to lean body tissue ratio is at a healthy level. Looking down at your dog, you should be able to see a "waist," where there is an obvious indentation behind the ribs. Lightly rub your hands along the ribs: they should be obvious but not sticking out. If they are hard to feel, the dog is probably overweight. In addition, overweight dogs will have palpable fat in the groin area of the hind legs.

The obvious cure for obesity in dogs is to reduce caloric intake and increase activity. Be sure you do not do either of these to excess, as that could lead to additional health problems.

Microchips

A terrier that has a microchip embedded in the skin near the shoulder has a much better chance of finding its way home should it ever get lost and end up in a shelter or at a veterinarian's office. This high-tech device, about the size of a grain of uncooked rice, contains a number that can be accessed by a scanner. Dogs turned into rescue organizations, shelters, and veterinary offices are now routinely being checked for microchip information to help them get back to their owners.

The curious terrier nature can send this Norwich off in search of adventure; a microchip can help the owner find a lost wanderer.

Whenever your dog is outside, be sure the area is properly—and safely—fenced.

than 50 percent of dogs are being returned to owners in England, the success rate in the United States is at less than 20 percent. Hopefully these numbers will increase dramatically in the coming years.

Outdoor Housing

While most terriers are hardy by nature and could function in an outdoor kennel, the majority of today's terriers are kept as house pets. Although frail or ill dogs should never be exposed to extremes of weather, terriers on the whole should be given plenty of access to the outdoors. They are earth dogs and need time in the yard to express their instincts by digging in the dirt and exploring their environment.

Any dog that spends time outdoors requires proper protection from the elements. A proper-sized, well-constructed doghouse will provide adequate shelter against heat, cold, and dampness. The interior must be roomy enough to allow the dog to stretch out, but not too large to maintain warmth. A well-designed doghouse has a hinged top for ease of cleaning, and is well insulated and draftproof. The entrance should be just large enough to allow the dog to enter easily.

During the summer the house must be placed in a shaded area, while a sunny spot is best during cold periods. If possible, have the house sitting on a solid foundation other than earth. One possibility is to

The chip is safe and permanent. Implanting takes only a few seconds and is no more painful for the dog than a vaccination. Scanning the chip is painless. Best of all, this innovation is relatively inexpensive. The chip implantation usually costs from $20 (when adopting from a shelter) to $75 (private veterinarians). The information must be registered with a database, but most organizations handling this are charging only nominal fees. The American Kennel Club maintains a registry, with a cost of just $12.50 for the lifetime of the dog. Of course, it is the owner's responsibility to update address information any time there is a change.

The use of the microchip is increasing, but slowly. While more place the house on blocks to stand several inches off the ground. This allows air to flow underneath and prevents direct contact with the soil.

Any area where a terrier is allowed to roam freely should be properly fenced. As terriers are avid diggers, the fence must be deeply set to thwart the dog's ability to tunnel under it and escape. The doghouse should of course be positioned so that the dog cannot climb upon it and use it to jump over the fence.

Traveling with Your Terrier

Terriers are very people-oriented and will usually prefer to accompany you than to stay home alone. From the time the dog is a puppy you should accustom it to riding in the car. You can begin with short trips, such as local errands, and increase from there. The dog should always be placed in the back seat, and it should be lying down or in its crate when the car is in motion. Harnesses are available from dog specialty shops that allow you to loosely tether the dog to the seat belt attachment for safety.

In mild weather keep the car windows open approximately two inches during the ride to improve air circulation. Never allow the dog to hang its head out the window while the car is in motion, as this can result in eye, ear, and throat injuries.

During hot periods, provide the dog with a small amount of water at

A well-constructed dog house allows the dog some freedom of movement, is draft-free, and can be easily cleaned.

regular intervals to prevent dehydration when traveling without air conditioning. *Never leave a dog unattended in a parked car during the heat of the day.* Even with the windows slightly lowered, the internal temperature of the car can soar in just minutes and prove fatal to the trapped dog.

If your dog is prone to vomiting in the car and you are planning an extended ride, consult your veterinarian about medications to help alleviate the dog's nausea. Most dogs outgrow this tendency toward motion sickness as they get more accustomed to car trips. On long trips, plan to stop every two hours to allow the dog to relieve itself and get some exercise. It is especially important to remember to keep the dog on leash during these stops in unfamiliar terrain, where your terrier may bolt and get lost.

If your trip requires overnight lodging, be sure to carefully plan where you will be staying and make

The American Staffordshire Terrier is rugged and ready for anything.

advance reservations, as many facilities will not allow dogs. Travel guides and your local automobile club may be able to supply you with a useful list of places that will allow animals.

Whenever traveling with a dog, take along an adequate supply of the dog's normal food. This helps reduce the chance of digestive upset from a sudden new diet. When the animal is already faced with so many new experiences, having a reliable supply of food is a good preventive measure.

If you are unable to bring your dog with you on your travels, you will need to find good accommodations for your pet while you are away. The best solution is to have as caretaker someone the dog is familiar with. I've been using a pet-sitting service for a number of years, and my dogs seem to cope with my "disappearance" much better this way. My sitter visits three times a day, playing with them as well as feeding and attending to their elimination needs.

If this is not possible, you have several options to consider. The breeder from whom you purchased the dog may be in a position to board it temporarily; the pluses of this are the familiarity the breeder would have with the individual dog and the particular requirements and traits of the breed.

Commercial kennels routinely offer boarding services. Most are well run, clean, and attentive to the dog's basic needs. Before leaving your dog at a kennel, however, be sure to visit it and view the facility. If all seems in order, check that it is ac-credited by the American Boarding Kennel Association (ABKA). A list of approved kennels in your area can be obtained by writing the ABKA at 1702 East Pikes Peak Avenue, Colorado Springs, Colorado 80909 (*www.abka.com*; 719-667-1600). Once a kennel has been selected, leave enough of the dog's normal food to last until your return.

Air travel for animals has improved greatly in the last few years; progressive legislation requires all animals to be shielded from extremes of temperature. In recent times, traveling in airplanes has become commonplace for show dogs and for planned matings that involve partners from various areas of the country. Place a copy of the dog's itinerary, and a list of emergency phone numbers, inside the crate. Arrange to have a supply of the dog's normal food delivered with the dog upon arrival.

A special restraint leash can be placed on the dog to keep it secure when riding in the car.

Chapter Five

Grooming Your Terrier

Covering the techniques required to groom the group of terriers included in this book would require a book of its own, so the focus here is on grooming basics. You can get in-depth advice on the special techniques of grooming your breed from your terrier's breeder, members of the local or national club, or a groomer that specializes in grooming terriers for the show ring.

Although the grooming needs of a Yorkshire Terrier are quite different than those of the Smooth Fox Terrier, all terriers need some type of grooming to keep them looking as they should, according to their breed type. Proper grooming promotes good health, good hygiene, and a good appearance.

Coat Care

In simplest terms, the coat is the hair covering a dog's skin. There are five basic types of coats: long, non-shedding, silky, wiry, and smooth. Regardless of type, regular brushing

For most terriers, grooming and trimming are facts of life.

keeps the coat looking good. For most dogs, brushing twice weekly is recommended, but daily brushing is the best, as it becomes routine for the dog.

Most terrier breeds have double coats, which means there is both an outer coat and an undercoat. Dogs that were developed to work in harsh climates generally have double coats, and this includes most terriers. The hard outer coat provides protection from weather and prey, and the undercoat provides insulation. These dogs have coarse outer (or guard) hairs on top of a soft, downy undercoat that consists of fine, soft hairs that are much shorter than the guard hairs. There are approximately three to five undercoat hairs gathered around each guard hair. Once the guard hair grows several inches, it dies. For most terriers, the dead hairs do not fall out and must either be clipped or pulled out.

The coats of wirehaired dogs (including the Airedale, Australian, Black Russian, Border, Cairn, Cesky, Glen of Imaal, Irish, Lakeland, the Schnauzers, Norfolk, Norwich, Scottish, Sealyham, Skye, Welsh,

Grooming is a fact of life for terriers, particularly long-coated breeds and their owners. Anyone considering any coated terrier should either be prepared to handle the grooming or make arrangements for the services of a qualified professional.

This Manchester terrier is being groomed with a hound glove.

West Highland White, and Wire Fox) must be kept from getting tangled with dead hairs. Regular brushing with a stiff brush will prevent the coat from matting and making the dog uncomfortable. Removing dead hairs also helps maintain good coat texture and color.

Many terriers have coats that must be shorn on a regular basis, as much as every two months (but usually every three or four months). This can be done several ways: manually stripping or plucking out the hairs, or using an electric clipper. Scissoring is also used to maintain the hairs around the eyes, anus, and feet (but using scissors on a dog is dangerous and should only be done by a professional). Most terriers that are not being shown are clipped, as this is the easiest thing to do.

Most owners opt to have their pet terriers clipped by a professional groomer (although owners can also do this at home once trained in proper procedure). In this technique, the coat is cut with electric clippers, providing a uniform coat length (as decided by the size of blade used). There are a number of "standard" cuts (puppy, schnauzer, terrier, poodle, utility, etc.) that are the stock and trade of professional groomers and suitable for pet dogs. Many terrier breeds have distinct looks, however, and you should advise your groomer if you want a cut that is specific for your dog.

While the clipping process is quicker and perhaps easier on the terrier than plucking or stripping, there

are some disadvantages to consider. The most obvious is that the clippers can nick or cut the dog, especially if the dog won't stand still during the process. If a blade gets too hot and touches the skin, the dog may develop a rash known as clipper burn. This will usually disappear in a day or two, with little irritation for the dog.

Clipping the coat tends to soften the texture of the hair, which increases the chances for matting as the hair gets longer. Clipping also removes much of the coat's natural dirt-repelling and waterproofing qualities. With the outer coat and undercoat cut to the same length, the coat will often appear lighter than its normal color. People sometimes have their dogs clipped because they believe it will make the dog feel cooler in the summer. Since it is actually not the outer coat but the undercoat that insulates the dog, removing the outer hair can often weaken the coat's natural ability to cool the dog.

Stripping or plucking the coat is manually removing the dead hair of the outer coat. Once a dog's coat is "blown," the hair can be pulled out with little or no discomfort for the dog—if performed properly. Stripping

While many terriers require closely trimmed coats, several hard-coated breeds—such as this Cairn as well as Scottish Terriers and West Highland White Terriers—require only "tidying" to keep the coats looking natural.

Stripping is done using either the forefinger and thumb or a tool called a stripping knife, which is used to improve the grip on the hairs being plucked out and acts as an extension of the fingers. A small number of hairs are collected between the thumb and the underside of the knife and pulled out, in a sharp, quick motion in the direction the coat grows. If done properly, this should be painless for the dog.

Hand stripping your dog is hard work and can be very time consuming, as much as five hours for an experienced groomer, so the dog will have to be trained from an early age to behave for long periods of time. Also, stripping a coat can be quite expensive if you cannot do it yourself, and it may be very difficult to find a groomer willing to do it. That is why many terrier owners learn the process for themselves.

helps retain the wiry texture of the terrier's coat, which in turn produces a harder, more colorful, and more dirt- and water-repellent coat.

A pin brush will help remove snarls in this Soft Coated Wheaten's coat.

Grooming Show Dogs

Grooming terriers for the show ring requires a great deal of time, as the dog must be perfectly sculptured according to the breed standard. All competitors undergo some judicious grooming before entering the show ring. Some terriers need extensive plucking and trimming, while others need only contouring and finishing.

For the owner of a breed that requires the coat to be plucked and stripped, this preparation begins months before the show date. In order to bring a terrier coat into good condition, the coat should be stripped at least six to eight weeks prior to the show. The coat of a show dog can never be clipped because it can take three months to reestablish correct coat texture. Repeated strippings of the coat will hopefully yield improved coat texture and lie of the hair; the new coat will come in harsher in texture and will lay tighter to the body, giving a clean, smooth appearance.

Show dogs should be groomed *before* being bathed. Grooming removes the unwanted hair and mats, which would block the shampoo from getting through the coat. Knots in the coat will only get worse and painful for the dog if not removed before bathing, as knotted hair twists and can pinch the skin when wet.

If the harsh-coated terrier must be bathed, it must be done far enough in advance of the show to allow the normal hardness of the coat to return. This generally takes about ten days. After bathing the dog, use a hair dryer with the lie of the hair and using a brush to dry the coat, making sure the hair is dry to the skin. Typically, only the longer "furnishings" are washed for a show.

Grooming Tools

Most of the basic grooming tools should be available in pet stores, but you may need to find a mail-order catalog that specializes in dog

Grooming for the show ring requires preparation that can take months. This champion Kerry Blue shows what it takes to win.

grooming equipment if your breed has special grooming requirements. The most common tools used on terriers are:

• **brushes** (pin brushes have straight metal pins in a cushioned backing and are used on long-haired breeds; palm pads are especially meant for use on terriers; slicker brushes have shorter metal pins that are sometimes bent at the ends and are good for all coats to remove shedding hairs)

• **clippers** (the size of the blade indicates the closeness of the cut; the higher the number, the closer the cut; clipper coolant also needed)

• **combs** (teeth of various widths available; get at least a fine, a coarse, and a flea comb; mat comb is used to remove coat mats)

• **ear cleaner** (liquid, use with cotton swabs)

Terrier coats come in many types and textures. Groomers require an array of grooming tools to deal with each breed's particular requirements. Pictured are various types of brushes, combs, hound gloves, clippers, and trimming aids.

- **grooming table** (must have a nonskid top, be sturdy, and be the correct height for the groomer; usually only necessary for people doing coat stripping/clipping or showing their dog)
- **nail clippers** ("guillotine" or scissors styles; electric versions also available)
- **scissors** (buy top-quality, which will not become dull quickly)
- **shampoo** (should be made for dogs only; bathe only when necessary)
- **styptic powder** (for use when nail quick is nicked and bleeds)
- **thinning shears** (single- or double-serrated for blending, smoothing, and reducing undercoat)
- **toothbrush and paste** (paste must be made for dogs, not humans; fingertip brush is most easily handled)

- **treats** (always reward your dog for good behavior and patience during the grooming process)

Bathing

Bathing should not be done too often, as it removes the natural oils from the coat and skin. In fact, I generally advise bathing only when your terrier has rolled in something that can't be combed out. Bathing creates a need for more bathing, in a way. The chemicals in shampoos dry and damage the hair shafts. Damaged hair, in turn, attracts dirt and oil, which leads to odor. Smelly terriers need to be bathed, so the circle is complete.

If you must bathe your terrier, be sure to use a shampoo that is specially designed for dogs, and preferably for terriers (you can find these in specialty catalogs). A dog's coat has a different pH level than human hair, and using a shampoo designed for humans can leave your dog with dry, itchy, flaking skin. At best, all shampoos remove some of the coat's natural oils, thereby affecting the coat's ability to waterproof and insulate the dog.

Clipping Nails

The nails of the working terrier were never a problem, as the dog would wear them down during its daily activity on rough terrain. Today's terriers are predominantly housepets, so there is little natural wearing down of the nails. Unclipped toenails continue to grow and will eventually curve down toward the ground. Left uncorrected, this will force the foot up, forcing the dog to walk awkwardly. Ultimately, the Achilles tendons can be stretched, causing muscle strains and cramps. Also, overly long nails can be dangerous, as they can catch on a rough surface and be ripped off, causing serious injury. Few terriers' nails ever come near this point, as most owners will quickly tire of being a human pincushion when their little love jumps on them.

If your terrier goes to a groomer, you will probably never have to deal with clipping its nails, as this is included in the grooming package. The technicians at your veterinarian are also expert at this procedure, and you might want to let them handle it, as most terriers *hate* to have their nails clipped. In fact, I have one dog that is so sensitive to this that the last time I had him at the veterinarian, it took three people to subdue him to the point where the clipping was possible (that was $13 well spent, in my opinion).

Various tools can be used, including electric or scissors types, but I find the guillotine-type clipper the most efficient. Be sure the blade is very sharp, and cut on a slight angle toward the footpad.

If you are doing the procedure yourself, remember that you must be careful not to cut through the quick,

This Boston Terrier's nails are being clipped using a "guillotine" clipper.

which is the blood supply to the nail. The knack is to get as close to the quick as possible without hitting it. If your dog is cooperative, you can remove small amounts of nail and continue until you will see a small red dot in the center of the nail (that's the quick). If you accidentally go too far, the bleeding is usually easily stopped with styptic powder, nail clotting powder, or some cotton applied with pressure to the end of the nail. After the toenails have been trimmed, and your dog is still cooperating, use a small scissor to round off the hair on the feet and trim the hairs between the pads.

Chapter Six

Health Care

On the whole, terriers are a rugged group not prone to many out-of-the-ordinary illnesses. This hardiness should not be taken for granted; it hinges on good everyday care, the availability of a nutritious diet, and ample exercise. In addition, every dog needs routine veterinary checkups and required vaccinations throughout its life. I cannot recommend too strongly that you consult a veterinarian shortly after you notice symptoms of illness in your terrier. Delaying treatment can be a costly mistake. Many illnesses that are easily handled in the early stages can become life-threatening if treatment is delayed.

Medical Disorders in Terriers

The list that follows contains descriptions of diseases and disorders that can afflict terriers. Most of these are quite rare. Terriers are generally very hardy, long-lived dogs, but—like any group of pure-bred dogs—they are bred from a limited gene pool, which makes them susceptible to carrying and passing on certain genetic disorders to their offspring. Breeds that are more prone to certain disorders than other terriers are shown in parentheses at the end of the definition.

Aberrant cilia: abnormal growth of the eyelashes, usually causing an abrasion of the eyeball.

Acrodermatitis: hereditary disorder in which a puppy's immune system cannot properly metabolize zinc; these puppies are usually underdeveloped and die within several weeks of birth.

Addison's disease (hypoadrenocorticism): loss of function of the adrenal glands, leading to abnormal levels of sodium, potassium, and glucose in the blood. The disease is thought to be an autoimmune disorder.

Allergic dermatitis: skin disease caused by an allergic reaction to flea bites.

Atopic dermatitis: skin disease, commonly known as "atopy," thought

Exercise is a vital part of a healthy terrier's life.

Even apparently healthy terriers need an annual medical evaluation by a veterinarian.

to be genetic. It is caused by an allergic reaction to substances in the environment that are either absorbed through the skin or inhaled. Symptoms usually begin by one year of age, with the worst outbreaks during the summer months, but can occur year round. Atopy causes intense itching, particularly around the paws; the skin may be red and irritated due to scratching, and may eventually bleed and become infected. The ears may also be irritated. Food allergies can be misdiagnosed as atopy.

Autoimmune diseases: immune system defect whereby it attacks and rejects the body's own tissue as foreign, often causing damage, typi-

cally to the thyroid, kidneys, or lungs. *See* Addison's disease.

Cardiomyopathy: condition where the heart becomes enlarged (dilated), which leads to an impaired ability to pump blood (also known as dilated cardiomyopathy).

Cataracts: clouding of the ocular lens of the eye. Degenerative cataracts result from an injury or systemic disease. Juvenile cataracts occur in young dogs and are inherited by receiving autosomal recessive genes from both carrier parents. Most cataracts get progressively worse and may eventually result in blindness. Surgery is indicated for severely affected dogs. Potential breeding stock should be evaluated for this condition by the Canine Eye Registration Foundation, which will issue a clearance certificate for all unaffected dogs. (Bedlington, Boston, Wire Fox, Parson Russell, Scottish, Soft Coated Wheaten, Staffordshire Bull, West Highland White, and Yorkshire Terriers; Miniature Schnauzer)

Cerebellar hypoplasia: condition where the cerebellum of the brain is too small and does not function properly.

Copper toxicosis: genetic disorder that affects the liver's ability to excrete excess dietary copper, leading to liver failure. (Bedlington Terrier)

Craniomandibular osteopathy: abnormal development of the bones of the jaw and face, usually appearing at about six months of age. Symptoms include lack of appetite or inability to eat, fever, lethargy, and pain when mouth is examined. This is a hereditary disorder that is usually curable with medication. (Cairn Terrier, West Highland White Terrier)

Cryptorchidism: condition where one or both testicles do not descend into the scrotum sac. This can be repaired by surgery, but neutering is the usual treatment.

Cushing's syndrome: hormonal disorder caused by an excess of the hormone cortisol, usually caused by a tumor on the pituitary or adrenal glands. Symptoms are increased thirst and urination, coat problems, and a pot belly. This disorder is closely linked with diabetes and can be controlled with medication. (Scottish Terrier)

Deafness: the inability to hear, in one or both ears. Neurologic (sensorineural) deafness is often hereditary, caused by abnormalities of the inner ear or auditory nerve. Conduction deafness is caused by severe infections or injury to the ear.

Demodectic mange: genetic skin disorder resulting from stress on the immune system, usually during adolescence. It is most often seen as a few small patches on the head or body. (Bull Terrier)

Diabetes: the inability to absorb sugar from the blood caused by insufficient production of the hormone insulin by the pancreas. Symptoms include increased thirst, hunger, and urine production, with vomiting, dehydration, and eventually coma in latter stages. This can be controlled with medication. (Miniature Schnauzer)

Elbow dysplasia: degenerative disease of the elbow of dogs, usually

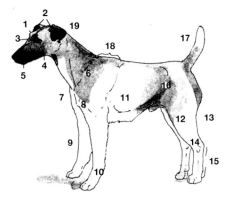

The structure of a Smooth Fox Terrier. Knowledge of your pet's external and internal anatomy will help you communicate with your veterinarian.

1. skull
2. ears
3. stop
4. cheek
5. muzzle
6. shoulder
7. chest
8. brisket
9. forequarters
10. front pastern
11. ribcage
12. stifle
13. hindquarters
14. hock
15. rear pastern
16. loin
17. tail
18. withers
19. neckline

genetic. Three or more conditions make up this disease, and they can occur independently or in conjunction. Symptoms include pain, lameness, and changes in gait. *See also* Hip dysplasia. (American Staffordshire Terrier)

Epilepsy: seizure or "fit," caused by a number of conditions, including brain tumor, hypoglycemia (low blood sugar), heat stroke, hypothyroidism, poisoning, and distemper. There are two types of epilepsy. Secondary epilepsy is when a specific cause for the seizures can be found. Idiopathic epilepsy, also called primary or hereditary epilepsy, is when the cause is unknown. Idiopathic

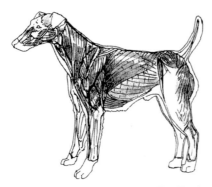
The musculature of a Smooth Fox Terrier.

epilepsy usually begins in adult dogs, between three and five years of age. During a seizure the dog's limbs stiffen, pupils dilate, and there is excess salivation. Seizures usually last only a minute or two, but they may become longer and more frequent in severely affected dogs. Medication is used to control epilepsy only when the seizures are frequent. (Scottish Terrier)

Factor VIII deficiency: *See* Hemophilia.

Factor IX deficiency: *See* Hemophilia.

Glaucoma: abnormally high fluid pressure in the eye. It is the leading cause of blindness in dogs. If this pressure cannot be reduced, the retina and optic nerves will be permanently damaged. Glaucoma is usually inherited, but it can also be caused by luxation of the lens, tumors of the eye, and other secondary diseases. Affected dogs are usually treated by medicine and surgery, if severe. *See also* Lens luxation. (Boston, Dandie Dinmont, and Fox Terriers; Miniature Schnauzer)

Globoid cell leukodystrophy (GCL): fatal, autosomal recessive disease caused by a deficiency of an enzyme controlling metabolic processes. Also known as Krabbe's disease, GCL is termed a "storage" disease, where an abnormal amount of cells accumulate in the brain. Symptoms include weakness, tremors, difficulty walking, and slow growth. (Cairn Terrier, West Highland White Terrier)

Hemophilia: bleeding disorder caused by a deficiency in specific coagulation factors. Hemophilia A, also known as factor VIII deficiency, is the most common type of hemophilia in dogs. Hemophilia B, also known as factor IX deficiency or Christmas disease, is rare and results from a lack of coagulation factor IX. Hemophilia is a sex-linked recessive disorder that is carried by females and manifested in males (although females with two affected X chromosomes can also develop the disease). This is a lifelong problem that will require protective measures to avoid injury, and blood transfusions may be required.

Hepatic portosystemic shunt: *See* Liver shunt.

Hernia: rips in the muscle wall that allow body organs and tissue to bulge into areas where they do not belong. The two most common hernias in dogs are umbilical (in the navel) and inguinal (in the groin). If a hernia can be pushed back in it is called reducible; hernias that cannot be reduced are called incarcerated. If an incarcerated hernia loses its

With proper amounts of exercise and medical care, these Manchester Terriers should live long, healthy lives.

blood supply, the hernia becomes strangulated, which is an emergency situation. Most hernias reduce gradually and eventually disappear, but some will need surgery to correct.

Hip dysplasia (HD): congenital malformation of the hip joint, where the head of the femur (thigh bone) does not fit properly in the hip socket, resulting in arthritis, pain, and lameness in the hindquarters. Also known as degenerative joint disease, hip dysplasia begins as damage to the cartilage lining the hip joint, which reduces lubrication, and the joint eventually degrades to

where the dog's range of motion is impeded. The disease can be aggravated by obesity; excess protein, calcium, and/or calories in the diet; and too much exercise. There are many degrees of severity, and the pain of the resulting arthritis can be relieved with anti-inflammatory medications and pain relievers. Surgery is often performed on young adults and can range from partial to total hip replacement or pelvic surgery to tighten the socket/femur fit. Since this disease is hereditary, any dog being used for breeding should have its hips x-rayed at approximately 12 to 16 months of age. The films should be sent to the Orthopedic Foundation for Animals for evaluation. Only those dogs certified as clear should be used for breeding. *See also* Elbow dysplasia. (American Staffordshire Terrier, Giant Schnauzer, Staffordshire Bull Terrier)

Hyperadrenocorticism: *See* Addison's disease, Cushing's syndrome.

Hypothyroidism: endocrine disease where the thyroid gland produces an abnormally low amount of hormones. It is the most frequent hormone imbalance in dogs and is most commonly caused by an autoimmune destruction of the thyroid gland. Symptoms include fatigue, hair loss, weight gain, chronic skin infections, intolerance to cold, and infertility. The condition is usually controllable by daily medication.

Juvenile cataracts: *See* Cataracts.

Keratoconjunctivitis sicca (KCS): also known as "dry eye," persistent dryness of the cornea and conjunctiva (the membranes of the

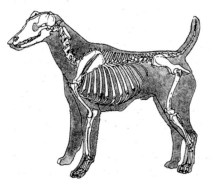

The skeleton of a Smooth Fox Terrier.

eye socket) caused by decreased output of the tear glands or increased evaporation of tears. Without tears, eyes become irritated, the white of the eyes gets red, the cornea in time will turn brown, and a gooey, yellow discharge will develop. In the early stages, the dog will blink a lot, the eye will look dull, and the dog will avoid bright light. Blindness can result if left untreated. Congenital KCS is rare but has been seen in the Yorkshire Terrier; afflicted dogs are born with no tear-producing glands or ones that are abnormally small. Prescription medication and artificial tears, applied four to six times daily, are commonly used to relieve this condition. (Boston, Bull, Kerry Blue, Sealyham, West Highland White, and Yorkshire Terriers; Miniature and Standard Schnauzers)

Legg-Perthes disease: also known as Legg-Calve-Perthes disease, a relatively common disease of the hip joint in small terrier breeds, often referred to as the small dog's hip dysplasia. It is thought to be genetic and is usually seen in dogs from three to thirteen months of age. It is caused by a degeneration of the hip joint when blood stops flowing in the femoral artery. Symptoms include limping, pain, and eventually arthritis in the hindquarters. It is treated surgically. (Border, Lakeland, Parson Russell, and Soft Coated Wheaten Terriers)

Lens luxation: painful condition where the lens in the eye is moved into an abnormal position. This dislocation of the lens may result from

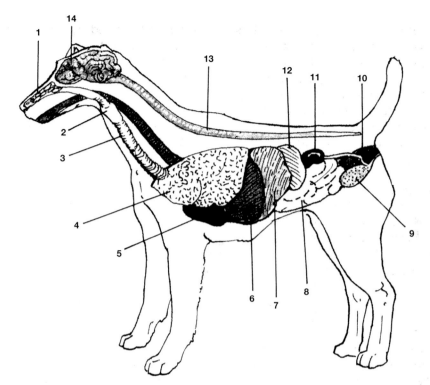

Internal organs (a Smooth Fox Terrier is used for this demonstration).

1. sinus cavity
2. thyroid cartilage
3. trachea
4. lungs
5. heart
6. liver
7. stomach
8. small intestine
9. bladder
10. rectum
11. kidneys
12. spleen
13. spinal column
14. brain

trauma, but it is usually a genetic condition that leads to glaucoma and an eventual loss of vision. Surgery to remove the lens sometimes will restore at least partial vision, but this condition must be caught early for treatment to be effective. (Bedlington, Fox, Manchester, Miniature Bull, Parson Russell, Scottish, Welsh, and West Highland White Terriers)

Liver shunt: congenital malformation of the blood vessels in the liver. Affected puppies are small and do not gain weight. They appear listless, weak, and may vomit or have seizures. These problems appear worse shortly after eating. This condition can be diagnosed by a bile acid test and usually can be corrected by surgery. (Scottish Terrier, Yorkshire Terrier)

Mycobacterium avium infection: illness similar to tuberculosis that is spread by contact with infected bird droppings or contaminated water. This infection is hard to diagnose, and symptoms are diarrhea, vomiting, weakness, loss of appetite, and extremely swollen lymph nodes. The lymph nodes are

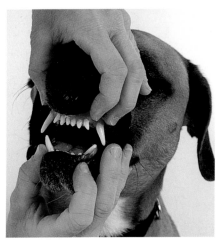

Your veterinarian will check the dog's bite, teeth, and gums at the annual checkup and will advise you if the teeth need scaling.

the primary point of infection, and a misdiagnosis of lymphatic cancer may be made. (Miniature Schnauzer)

Obsessive-compulsive disorder (OCD): condition where a normal behavior is repeated constantly, to the point of self-mutilation or exhaustion. Common obsessive behaviors include tail chasing (spinning), licking, chasing light or shadows, and digging. Pica is a compulsion to eat inappropriate items, which can cause life-threatening intestinal blockages. OCD in dogs is believed to be genetic and can be controlled by daily medication. (Bull Terrier, Parson Russell Terrier)

Patellar luxation: recurring dislocation (slipping in and out of place) of the kneecap, causing pain and lameness. This congenital condition is also known as "slipped stifles." Symptoms include a quick change in gait, from apparently normal movement to carrying a hind limb off the ground the next minute. Surgery can usually correct the problem as long as the kneecap hasn't degenerated too much. (Border, Bull, and Yorkshire Terriers)

Progressive retinal atrophy (PRA): inherited, incurable eye disease where the retina slowly deteriorates, producing night blindness and eventually total blindness. There are two main forms of PRA. Primary retinal dystrophy is progressive and will eventually result in total blindness. Dogs with central progressive atrophy have better vision in dim light than in bright light because of a blind patch in their central field of vision. This form of PRA is also progressive but may not produce total blindness. (Miniature Schnauzer, Parson Russell Terrier)

Retinal dysplasia: condition where the retina (located at the back of the eye) is malformed. The condition is usually genetic and not progressive, so the dog's condition at birth will rarely deteriorate or improve. The condition can also be caused by a viral infection in the mother prior to birth. (Bedlington, Sealyham, and Yorkshire Terriers)

Scottie cramp: hereditary disorder most commonly found in Scottish Terriers. An afflicted dog's normal gait is impeded when the dog becomes overstimulated or excited. The dog's legs "cramp," but there is no loss of consciousness or seizure, and the symptoms quickly disappear as the level of excitement decreases.

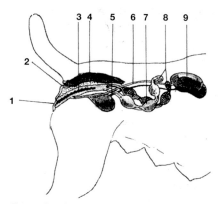

Reproductive system of the female:

1. vulva
2. anus
3. vagina
4. rectum
5. bladder
6. ureter
7. developing embryo
8. ovaries
9. kidneys

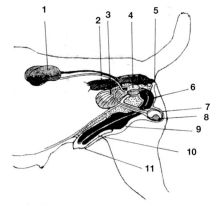

Reproductive system of the male:

1. kidneys
2. rectum
3. bladder
4. prostate
5. anus
6. urethra
7. scrotum
8. testes
9. bulb
10. penis
11. sheath

Von Willebrand's disease (VWD): the most common inherited bleeding disorder in dogs, caused by the lack of von Willebrand factor (a clotting factor) in the blood. It is less severe than hemophilia. Symptoms include easy bruising, excessive bleeding during surgery, bleeding from the nose or gums during teething, blood in the stools or urine, and heavy bleeding during the bitch's heat cycle and after whelping. VWD can be diagnosed with a blood test, and all affected and carrier animals should not be used for breeding. This disorder can be brought on by hypothyroidism and improved by medication in those cases, but in many dogs there is no effective treatment. (Kerry Blue, Manchester, and Scottish Terriers; Miniature Schnauzer)

Routine Care

Your terrier should receive a routine, annual checkup, even when young and apparently healthy. State-of-the-art veterinary care can catch illnesses when they are still easily cured, and preventive medicine can extend your dog's life. Such care is not cheap, however. There are now organizations offering "pet insurance" that may help owners afford the veterinary care their pets need. One such organization is Veterinary Pet Insurance (800-USA-PETS, *www.petinsurance.com*). Many veterinarians also offer comprehensive plans where they bundle routine procedures together and offer them at a reduced rate.

Problems that are caught promptly are usually much easier to deal with, so be on the lookout for the early stages of disorders. The eyes, ears, and feet are particularly vulnerable in terriers, as these body parts often get right in on the digging and hunting actions that delight terriers.

Conscientious owners monitor the overall health of their pets by regularly inspecting exposed areas (eyes, ears, feet, skin, and teeth) for signs of discharge, abrasions, or sensitivity. This should become a regular routine during the grooming process. Begin by running your hands over the dog's entire body and feeling for anything unusual, such as cysts, sores, and areas that are swollen or cause the dog pain when touched. For breeds with tough double coats, be sure to get down to the skin and look and feel for signs of irritation. Next, you should turn to the head and begin a more thorough examination.

Ears

The ears should be routinely inspected for foreign objects (dirt, burrs, bugs) and scratches. Symptoms of ear problems are a constant shaking of the head, rubbing the ears (with the paws or on the ground), excessive earwax, redness, swelling, or a foul odor from the ear canal. These symptoms will require a veterinarian's attention.

You can see into the dog's ear by using a small flashlight, but *never* probe inside the ear canal; this can be extremely painful for the dog and can greatly damage this very sensitive organ. To reduce the normal buildup of wax and dirt in the ear,

routinely swab the easily reached areas with a cotton ball dampened with warm water. If cleanliness is a continual problem, ointments made specially for cleaning the *outer* ear can be bought from pet shops, grooming parlors, or your veterinarian. Avoid oily compounds; their sticky residue may, in fact, *attract and retain* dirt. If you suspect that the ear is heavily laden with wax, let your veterinarian do a more thorough cleaning. If the problem is chronic, ask for instructions to perform this procedure at home.

The most common ear irritations are simple abrasions, which will require a salve to reduce the sting and promote healing. Your veterinarian can tell you what salve to apply.

If your terrier shows increased sensitivity when you touch its ears, an infection may be present.

Otitis, an inflammation of the inner or outer ear, can be treated locally. Possible causes of the inflammation are parasites (such as mites) or bacteria. For appropriate treatment, accurate diagnosis is required, so seek veterinary assistance at first sign of a problem. Do not use over-the-counter ointments unless so instructed by your veterinarian. Deafness can be the tragic result of incorrectly treated or untreated ear infections.

Eyes

It is not uncommon for some terriers to produce a slight discharge around the eyes that can be easily cleared away with a damp, lint-free cloth. If this discharge becomes excessive, or if your dog blinks constantly and one or both eyes are red, consult your veterinarian. Small external eye lesions may be caused by low vegetation, and minor internal irritations may result when tiny particles are caught under the eyelids. These occurrences will normally be slightly painful for the dog and any scratches should quickly heal without treatment. Minor irritations can quickly become serious, however, so special attention should be paid to a constant discharge or pawing of the eye area.

Feet

Working terriers (and those pets that *feel* like working terriers) do a great deal of digging, which makes their paws susceptible to various minor injuries. The pads of your terrier's feet should be inspected regularly, especially if the dog limps or favors a leg. Burrs, splinters, or stones can become caught in and between the pads of the foot, and scratches are quite common. For minor problems, a cleaning with warm soapy water may be sufficient. If necessary, use sterilized tweezers to remove foreign objects, and apply a mild antiseptic.

If your dog suddenly begins to limp and favor or lick one foot, an insect bite could be the cause. If you suspect this, apply an ice compress to reduce or prevent swelling and ease the pain. Unless there is an allergic reaction (see "Stinging Insects," page 84), this condition should pass quickly.

If there is no evidence of a cut or sting, and the dog indicates pain in the foot, there may be an injury to the bones or muscles of the area or there may be an object deeply embedded in the footpad. Both these conditions require diagnosis by a veterinarian.

If you live in a snowy climate, you need to protect your dog's feet from snow-melting chemicals on sidewalks, as these are caustic to a dog's footpads and skin. When you return home after a walk, rinse your terrier's feet with warm, soapy water. Pay special attention to drying between the toes. Salts and sand caught in these spaces by the short, matted hairs will lead to painful irritations. A little talcum powder will help, also. When thoroughly dry, apply a thin layer of petroleum jelly to soothe any irritation. Remember, too, that if bothered by these chemicals, the dog might lick its feet to relieve discomfort. Ingesting such poisonous materials is, of course, hazardous to your pet's health.

Simple Health Care Procedures

There are a number of simple procedures that every dog owner should master. These include taking a dog's temperature and pulse, and giving it medication.

Taking the Temperature

A dog's normal temperature is slightly higher than a human's—100°

When taking a dog's temperature, be sure the dog is properly restrained to avoid any possible injury.

to 101.5°F (37.7–38°C). Begin by lubricating the end of a heavy duty rectal thermometer with a little petroleum jelly. It is best to have an assistant nearby to help restrain the dog during the insertion and to prevent the dog from injuring itself by sitting down or otherwise breaking

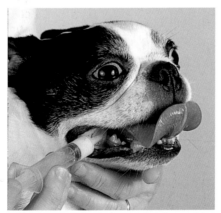

Liquid medication is best administered by using a syringe to deposit the medicine into the back of the mouth.

the thermometer. It is best to have the dog stand, but it can also lie on its side. One person should get a secure grasp on the dog while the other lifts the tail and inserts the thermometer. The thermometer should remain for two to three minutes for an accurate reading.

Giving Medication

Another procedure most dog owners have to face is giving their dog medication. There are several methods, depending on the type and amount of medicine required. Giving a dog a pill or capsule may seem simple enough, but more is required than just popping the pill into Rocco's mouth. Most dogs quickly master the technique for *not* swallowing pills, and defiantly spit them right out. The easiest (and sneakiest) method is to disguise the pill in something tasty, such as a small chunk of hamburger meat or a piece of cheese that is quickly swallowed in one gulp. If the dog swallows it happily, consider yourself lucky. If not, you will have to gently pry the dog's mouth open by applying pressure at the back of its jaws, tilt the head up *slightly*, and insert the pill as far back on the tongue as possible. Close the jaws and look for a swallow. Gently stroking the throat may help the cause. *Never lift the dog's head straight up; this can lead to having the pill inhaled into the windpipe rather than being swallowed.*

When administering liquid medicine, place it in a medicine spoon or syringe and pour it into the *back of the mouth* by lifting up the side of the dog's lower lip by the back molars and holding the head *slightly* upward. This allows the medicine to slide down the throat. Keep a grasp around the dog's muzzle until you are sure it has swallowed, or the dog may easily spit the medicine out. Again, never hold the head in an exaggerated upward position, as this invites choking.

Liquid and powdered medicines may also be mixed into the dog's food; check this with your veterinarian first, however. Many dogs spot the additives right away and won't touch the food. If this is the case, the powdered medications can usually be liquefied by adding a little water, and you can proceed as described above.

Taking the Pulse

A potentially lifesaving procedure you can easily perform is to monitor the dog's heartbeat. A dog's normal heartbeat is 70 to 90 beats per minute, but may vary with such factors as age, temperature, exertion, stress, and illness. A pulse can be found in the front paw, but the one located on the inside of the thigh is the easiest to read. Press softly against the pulse and monitor the pattern and rate of the beats. This procedure should be performed if you ever notice signs of extreme fatigue, fainting, or hyperactivity in your dog. Any abnormal patterns in

A muzzle can be applied to prevent a nervous dog from snapping when undergoing veterinary procedures.

the heartbeat require immediate attention by a veterinarian.

Common Illnesses

Most dogs contract a few minor illnesses in the course of their lives; these disorders will hopefully be no more serious than passing upsets in humans. Dogs, however, often cannot communicate their discomforts to their owners, so it is up to you to monitor your terrier's condition and decide whether veterinary attention is required.

Vomiting

Various illnesses that involve the digestive tract will lead to vomiting. Most incidents are quick to pass and are often related to something the dog has eaten. Severe, continued vomiting is very serious, however, and can lead to dehydration.

If the vomiting is limited to a few episodes, the first step is to withhold all food for 12 to 24 hours. You can administer some Pepto-Bismol to help settle the dog's stomach and

allow a few sips of water. If there is no sign of fever and the vomiting lets up, you can give the dog several small, bland meals during the next 24 hours. If the vomiting does not recur, the normal diet can be resumed the following day. If vomiting continues or intensifies, or if you notice any blood or worms in the vomit, get the dog to a veterinarian at first opportunity.

While terriers on the whole are not given to unusual eating patterns, some dogs have a tendency to gulp their food. This, in turn, may result in a sudden regurgitation of the meal due to the presence of too much air in the stomach. If your terrier is prone to this behavior, the best solution is to serve several small meals each day rather than one or two large ones, thereby limiting the amount of food in the stomach at any one time and the need to vomit.

Diarrhea

Like vomiting, a mild case of diarrhea may have many causes, most of which are not serious or life-threatening. As with vomiting, the first step is to withhold food for the next 12 to 24 hours to allow the system to rid itself of any offending material in the intestinal tract. A small amount of water is permissible, however, as is a dose of Kaopectate to help soothe the intestines. If symptoms do not worsen during the next 24 hours, the dog can be allowed several small, bland meals containing a binding agent such as rice or oatmeal.

If you ever notice a bloody discharge, or if the diarrhea does not stop, veterinary assistance is needed. Diarrhea combined with vomiting and/or a high fever can be symptoms of a serious problem, so do not delay in getting help from a trained professional.

Constipation

Constipation most often occurs when the dog undergoes a sudden dietary change. However, a dog that is confined for too long may also bring on this problem by restraining its natural urges to eliminate until given access to the proper site. In such cases, the problem is usually temporary and can generally be relieved by administering a mild laxative, such as milk of magnesia. Ask your veterinarian for the proper dosage, based on your dog's weight. If your terrier tends to be constipated, add a little extra roughage to the dog's normal diet to aid proper elimination. If the condition lingers, your veterinarian may suggest remedial use of a glycerine suppository or a warm water enema.

Constipation can be a serious problem if not relieved, and can be brought on by a variety of causes. Should you ever see the dog actively straining, crying out with pain, and not passing any excrement, seek professional care at once. The dog might have swallowed an object that is now lodged in the intestinal tract, causing a life-threatening situation. Alternatively, there could be a tumor or other growth in the intestines. Such situations are emergencies that require specialized veterinary care.

Anal Gland Disorders

At the base of the dog's anus are two glands that secrete a strong smelling substance used by the dog as a scent marker. These glands, sometimes referred to as the "stink glands," are normally emptied during defecation. If, however, the glands are not completely cleared by the normal elimination process, they can become impacted and swollen, requiring manual emptying. The symptoms of impacted anal glands include a constant licking of the area and/or dragging the anus across the ground or floor. (This is also symptomatic of worm infestation.) If the anal glands appear full, they can be manually expressed by carefully pressing along the outsides of the sac with your thumb and forefinger positioned on either side of the gland. Be sure to hold several layers of toilet tissue over and below the gland to collect the fluid that comes out. If this procedure seems painful to the dog, or if there is any pus or blood mixed with the fluid, there is most likely an infection that will require veterinary attention. Wash the anal area with soapy water when finished.

The testicles should also be routinely inspected. An inflammation of the area, termed orchitis, may result from an injury to the testicle or an internal disorder. Left unchecked sterility can result. If the testicles appear enlarged, feel hard, or are painful for the dog (as evidenced by an unusual method of walking or sitting), immediate veterinary care is in order.

Examinations and Vaccinations

Regardless of the condition of your dog, it should get an annual physical examination by your veterinarian, who will evaluate the dog's general condition, test for internal parasites, and determine if the dog needs any inoculations. By keeping current with the required vaccinations you can protect your dog from many of the infectious diseases that have

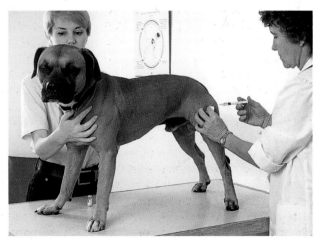

Maintaining a regular schedule of vaccinations will help ensure your pet's continued health.

proven to be killers. Most puppies receive their first immunizations while still with their breeder. These include, at around five to eight weeks of life, initial vaccinations for distemper, hepatitis, parvovirus, leptospirosis, and parainfluenza. A follow-up series will be required for most vaccines, on a schedule devised by your veterinarian. A rabies vaccination will also be needed, as well as boosters as the dog matures to help insure continued immunity.

Be sure to get from the breeder the records of your dog's earliest shots and pass this information along to your veterinarian. This is vital information for your dog's health record. At the initial checkup and then annually the dog may be tested for the presence of worms, and treated if necessary. Ask the breeder if the dog has already been tested and treated for worms. If it has, find out what type of worm the dog was infected with, what medication was used to treat it, and how the dog reacted to the medication. Worms are very common in puppies, and this background information can be very helpful in accurately assessing the dog's health.

Internal Parasites

As mentioned, worms are very common in dogs, especially puppies. Worms should never be ignored, however; left unchecked, worms can be very debilitating and sometimes life-threatening. Diagnos-

ing the type of worm present in a dog and devising the remedy should be left strictly to the veterinarian. Routine wormings of a dog using over-the-counter preparations are unnecessary and can be extremely dangerous.

Symptoms of worm infestation include weight loss, weakness, a bloated stomach, diarrhea, poor coat sheen, vomiting, anemia, loss of appetite, or, alternatively, a voracious appetite. The dog may exhibit signs of distress such as dragging its anus across the ground, or licking and biting around the tail area. Some infected dogs will give little outward sign of the problem until heavily infested, which points out the importance of having the dog checked at least annually.

Detecting the presence of most worms is done by microscopic examination of stool or blood samples. The most common types of worm are the roundworm, tapeworm, and hookworm, which live in the intestines.

The most important point to remember about worming is that a proper diagnosis by an expert and the administration of the proper medication in the proper dosage are the keys to eliminating the problem. Indiscriminately worming a dog can be deadly; all too frequently well-intentioned owners overdose their pets.

Heartworms

Heartworm disease is a potentially fatal disease caused by a worm called *Dirofilaria immitis*. The disease is spread by mosquitoes, which bite an infected dog, suck in the baby worms (microfilariae) floating in the bloodstream, and later return new larvae to another dog through a bite. The infected larvae travel through the bloodstream to the heart and adjacent veins, where they grow to maturity over the next few months. Female worms can grow to 14 inches (33 cm) in length; males are about half that size. A severely infected dog can have 300 or more worms.

Signs of heartworm infection are only seen after the infection is acute. Symptoms include weight loss, coughing, anemia, dull coat, lack of energy, difficulty breathing, fainting spells, and an enlarged abdomen. Advanced cases will yield damage to the heart, lungs, liver, and kidneys.

There are two types of heartworm tests: a screening test, which detects microfilaria circulating in the bloodstream, and a serology (or antigen) test, which checks for proteins in the bloodstream produced by adult heartworms. This second test is more sensitive and accurate, as approximately 20 percent of affected dogs will test negative because of an acquired immunity to the microfilaria stage of the heartworm.

The old adage "an ounce of prevention is worth a pound of cure" definitely applies to heartworms, as prevention is easy. In most cases, a once-monthly dose of medication is given, either taken as a tablet or used topically on the back. The most

The life cycle of the dog tapeworm: Tapeworm eggs are ingested by fleas and hatch in the fleas' intestines. Should a dog ingest an infected flea, the tapeworms mature in the dog's intestines. The mature tapeworms in turn lay eggs that are passed in the dog's stool. Tapeworm eggs can also be ingested by eating uncooked meat or fish.

popular products are ivermectin (Heartgard), milbemycin oxime (Interceptor and Sentinel), moxidectin (ProHeart), and topical selamectin (Revolution). A six-month injection of moxidectin (ProHeart6) is also available, as are diethycarbamazine tablets (Filarabits), which are given daily. You should decide with your veterinarian which method is best for you and your pet.

I've had recent experience with curing a dog with heartworm infestation. My daughter adopted an American Pit Bull Terrier mix from the local humane society, after the dog had apparently been used for breeding and then dumped in the streets. The shelter said it had tested Molly for heartworms and gotten a negative result. When Molly's coughing didn't subside despite several rounds of antibiotics, we brought her to a specialist. She had pneumonia and was treated for that, but still did not improve. It was not until Molly was coughing up large amounts of blood that they ran another heartworm test, which this time came up positive.

Because her infection was deemed severe, she had to have her curative shots in the reverse order (an initial dose to kill some of the worms, then two doses a month later to kill all that remained). During the treatment, Molly wasn't allowed any exercise or excitement, as an increased heart rate could lead to a possible heart attack or a clot forming in the lungs. It was touch and go for several weeks, but Molly pulled through. Ten years ago she probably would not have survived, as the new medications are less punishing on the body, but it was still a terrible ordeal for all involved (especially Molly). Now, every time I buy the monthly preventative for my three dogs, I think how great it is that they are protected.

Biting Bugs

There are numerous external parasites that can attack a dog. An owner's responsibility is to keep an eye on the dog's general health, paying close attention to the outward appearance of the coat, especially during the warm summer months. Infestations by lice or mites are not uncommon and can result in uncontrollable itching and scratching in afflicted dogs. This can lead to great damage to the dog's coat and skin that may take a long time to heal, so it is important to catch skin problems in the early stages. If you notice any clusters of eggs, a rash of bumps, or pustules on the skin, consult your veterinarian for proper diagnosis and treatment.

Fleas and ticks are a nasty fact of life. They infest a host, bite its skin, suck its blood, itch unbearably, and often infect the dog with tapeworm. Terriers are earth dogs, and external parasites will be found almost everywhere on earth that these dogs care to go. The severity of the problem may depend on the local climate and the type of coat the dog has. Breeds with wiry double coats may suffer from flea infestation and skin irritations without outward signs of the problems, so owners must be diligent to routinely inspect the dog's skin, especially if the dog is scratching or biting itself.

Fleas

Ridding a dog of fleas takes diligence. Powders and sprays designed especially for this purpose can be purchased at any pet store or grooming parlor. The coat must be thoroughly doused with the repellent in order for it to work; the active ingredient must reach the skin. Be extremely careful when applying the material, as it can do great damage to the dog's mucous membranes. Cover the dog's eyes, ears, nose, and mouth and slowly work the powder into the coat, working against the grain.

For heavy infestations, a bath with a flea dip will be needed. Many grooming parlors will do this as a service, or you can do it at home. Always use products designed just for this purpose, and read all directions before beginning.

Once the dog has been cleared of fleas, you will have to make sure that the house, especially the dog's bedding, is also free of parasites. If the fleas have found their way into the household carpeting, a heavy-duty insect bomb (available at most hardware stores and pet shops) will be needed to destroy all the breeding colonies.

These measures will temporarily take care of the problem, but the battle against fleas will usually go on as long as the weather sustains them.

Ticks

Ticks, another common problem for terriers, should not be taken lightly; they are disease carriers and can be painful for the afflicted dog. Once on their host, ticks gnaw through the skin and implant themselves so that they can suck and live off the dog's blood.

Removing a tick must be done carefully. If a tick is simply ripped from the skin, the head can tear away from the body and remain embedded in the skin. This often results in an infection or abscess. The proper way to remove a tick is to grasp it firmly, as close to the skin as possible, using a tweezer or your thumb and forefinger, and apply firm but gentle upward pressure. Do not twist. An alternative method is to apply a tick dip, which can be purchased from most veterinarians or pet shops. This will, in effect, suffocate the tick and make it release its hold on the dog's skin. *Never try to burn off a tick with a match or a cigarette.* The dangers of this should be evident. Once a tick has been removed, a small lump or swollen area may remain for several days.

Lyme Disease

Active, outdoor dogs like terriers can fall victim to Lyme disease. Technically a bacterial infection (*Borrelia burgdorferi*), it is transmitted through the bite of a tiny tick (*Ixodes scapularis*), commonly called the deer tick, which gets the bacteria from the white-footed mouse.

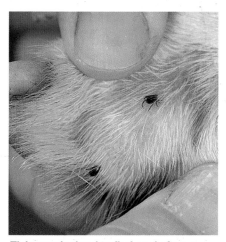

Ticks can be hard to find, and often establish themselves between a dog's toes.

Cases of Lyme disease have been found throughout the United States, but the disease is widespread in the Northeast, the upper Mississippi region, California, and certain southern states.

For the tick to transmit the bacteria into the dog's bloodstream, it must remain attached to the skin for at least one to two days. Since these ticks are smaller than the head of a pin, and they don't make the dog itch, they usually go unnoticed. The primary sign of infection is limping (usually one foreleg), which progresses over several days; it can start as mild and advance to where the dog may be unable to walk due to the joint pain. The afflicted dog will likely also have swollen lymph nodes in the affected limb, an elevated temperature, and little appetite.

Diagnosis is made by blood test, but many veterinarians will start the dog on antibiotics (usually one of the tetracyclines) even before the results are in. The antibiotic must be given for at least three or four weeks, and additional medication may also be prescribed for pain. The dog should show signs of recovery in two to three days.

Most dogs treated during the early stages of Lyme disease will respond rapidly to treatment and recover completely, but a few may be left with chronic joint pain. Left untreated, the bacteria can cause permanent joint damage and problems in the heart, kidneys, and nerve tissue. Approximately 5 percent of afflicted dogs will suffer a relapse and require another round of antibiotics, but it is not clear whether this is actually a flare-up of the original infection or a new occurrence.

Lyme disease cannot be transmitted by infected dogs to humans or other animals. A vaccine is now available to help prevent dogs from developing the disease, but its effectiveness is still being evaluated. One proven method of reducing the incidence of tick bite is monthly applications of anti-tick medication on the skin.

Stinging Insects

Bee and insect bites are generally difficult to detect. If you happen to witness your dog being bitten, check the site and see if the stinger is still embedded. If it is, carefully remove it by scraping your fingernail across the base of the bite using a scooping motion. This will limit the spread of the venom. If possible, apply ice or a cold compress to the area to reduce swelling and slow the flow of the toxin to other areas.

While a bug bite will usually be little more than a momentary discomfort for the dog, it can also be life-threatening. Occasionally, a dog will have an allergic reaction to a bite. Reactions will vary from dog to dog, depending on level of sensitivity. A case of hives or localized swelling will generally subside within hours, with no lasting effect. A more severe reaction, such as marked swelling or difficulty in breathing, requires immediate veterinary attention. For most cases, administering

Terriers thrive in the outdoors, which makes them susceptible to not only Lyme disease but also injuries from bites, cuts, and fractures.

some over-the-counter antihistamine (as advised by your veterinarian) or a corticosteroid will relieve symptoms. If your dog exhibits a marked tendency toward allergy to stinging insects, consult your veterinarian and devise a strategy for future emergencies, with antidotes available at all times.

Emergency Procedures

In emergencies speed is most important. If your dog sustains a serious injury, you must act quickly to stabilize the dog's condition until you can transport the animal to a veterinarian. Your first act must be to calm and restrain the dog. You cannot let the dog move about; this may lead to further damage. There may be internal problems not visible to the eye. You must also protect yourself from being bitten. The dog is terrified and may lash out at anyone that comes near it, so be sure to approach the animal carefully. Speak to it in low, soothing tones. A stocking, a tie, or a thin piece of cloth will serve as an emergency muzzle. Fold the material in half, placing the center fold on the top of the muzzle. Cross the two bands of material under the bottom of the jaw and bring them around to the back of the head. Tie a secure knot, but be sure it is not too restrictive. You are now ready to assess the dog's physical condition.

Wounds and Fractures

Never move an injured animal unless absolutely necessary, such as to remove it from a site where it may incur further damage. Inspect the skin and locate the source of any bleeding. If possible, gently wash the area with soap and warm water. If blood continues to flow, apply a clean cloth or gauze pad, secure it if possible, and hold the compress in place until the bleeding stops. Unless the cut is very small, it will need professional attention. A veterinarian will be better able to apply a bandage that will stay in place.

If it appears that a bone has been broken, immobilize the dog to the best of your ability. If allowed to move about, the dog may do damage to the muscles, cartilage, and nerves surrounding the break. Try to keep the dog calm and get it to emergency treatment as quickly as possible. If necessary, you can use a blanket as a makeshift stretcher for transporting the dog short distances.

If the dog lapses into unconsciousness, check that its breathing passages are open. Get the dog onto its side. Gently pry open its mouth and pull the tongue forward to allow air to flow into the lungs.

In all these situations, shock can quickly set in. Cover the dog with a blanket for added warmth and monitor its heart rate. This information may be useful for the attending veterinarian.

Poisonings

Most accidental poisonings occur without the owner ever knowing that the dog has ingested a poisonous substance. This often has serious consequences, since *immediate* action is generally required for the dog to have a good chance of survival. Symptoms of poisoning include diarrhea, vomiting, lethargy, spasms, shaking, dizziness, and a color change or bleeding of the mucous membranes.

If you know the cause of the poisoning and are lucky enough to have access to the packaging, look for information on the proper antidote. Your local poison control center may also be of help. Knowing how much poison was swallowed, and when, will greatly help your veterinarian to chart the treatment. Various procedures may be required, depending on the type of poison: sometimes the stomach can be pumped, sometimes specific antidotes can neutralize the poison in the stomach. Without adequate information on what happened, the veterinarian has little to go on and the outcome can be grave.

Terriers are inquisitive animals; this character trait can lead to trouble. Household items are the most common sources of poisoning, not only for children but also for housepets. Many house and garden plants are poisonous if chewed or eaten. Included among these are aloe vera, azalea, holly, philodendron, poinsettia, and daffodil bulbs. Keep locked up all cleaning agents, pesticides, and painting supplies. Antifreeze is particularly dangerous, as it is highly poisonous but has a pleasant odor and taste that attract the dog.

Chapter Seven

Descriptions of the Terrier Breeds

Airedale Terrier

The Airedale is the tallest member of the AKC Terrier Group. It was developed in the 19th century by the sportsmen of Yorkshire to assist in hunting fox, badger, otter, and other small game that inhabited the area. The early Airedales were noted for their keen eyesight, hearing, agility, and courage, but fell short of the otter hound in scenting and swimming ability. During the early formative period it is believed that otter hounds were occasionally crossed, and the result was a terrier of greater size and strength. Early names for the breed include the working terrier, the Waterside dog, and the Bingley Terrier.

Over the years the Airedale has developed into a dog of many talents. It has been used in Africa to assist in big-game hunting, and was one of the first breeds used for police work in Great Britain and Germany. It excels as a companion and is noted for its loyalty, high-spirited nature, and protectiveness toward home and master. It has a warm, loving disposition, but can be aloof to strangers and other animals.

The Airedale sports a wiry, double coat and is tan with a black saddle. It is muscular, weighing from 45 to 60 pounds (20.4–27.2 kg) on average, with an erect docked tail. The head is long and flat, with folded, V-shaped ears and dark, prominent eyes. Airedale litters range from five to ten puppies, with the newborns black at birth. The puppies develop the characteristic two-toned coat as they mature. The breed is quite hardy, although there is a tendency to hip dysplasia.

Airedales have been used for a wide variety of tasks including police work and hunting big game.

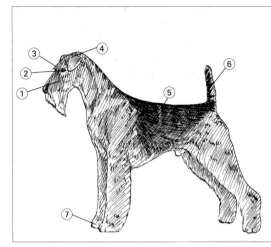

Illustrated Standard

1. Skull long and flat
2. Eyes small
3. Stop hardly visible
4. V-shaped ears with fold above the level of the skull
5. Back short and level
6. Tail set and carried high, of fair length
7. Feet small and round

❏ **Color:** tan with black or grizzle saddle

❏ **DQ:** none

The majestic Airedale Terrier has been dubbed the "King of Terriers."

Because of its size and strength, the Airedale requires an outlet for its energies and should be given regular thorough workouts. While the breed is suitable for apartment living, the dog must also be given ample access to the outdoors.

To reach its fullest potential, the Airedale needs a lot of human contact and adequate discipline from an early age. Left to its own devices, the

Airedale is willful enough to test the authority of its master, and must be reminded of its role as companion—not leader—in the household. Formal training in obedience methods is recommended. The Airedale thrives on human attention and develops a sweet disposition as it matures.

In the home the Airedale is a fine companion for all ages—strong and active enough to enjoy the rough play of youngsters and gentle enough to be trusted around small children. The Airedale is adaptable enough to accept other animals in the household, although it may be aggressive toward other male dogs.

The harsh, wiry coat of the Airedale must be combed and brushed several times a week and trimmed regularly to keep the dog looking tidy. Show dogs will require stripping and plucking, as clipping is not permissible and will damage the coat's desired texture. Bathing should be only as needed. During grooming and bathing inspect the skin for rashes or sores that might otherwise go undetected.

American Staffordshire Terrier

Take just one look at a well-bred American Staffordshire Terrier and the first impression will undoubtedly be one of strength and power. The breed dates to the late 19th century in the English countryside, where these dogs were developed as farm dogs and to bait bulls. Dogfighting was also a popular "sport," and the ancestors of these dogs developed a reputation for unmatched courage, loyalty, and aggressiveness.

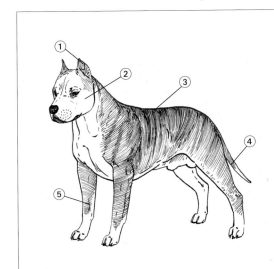

Illustrated Standard

① Ears set high, cropped or uncropped (preferred); uncropped ears short and held half rose or prick

② Head broad, pronounced cheek muscles, distinct stop

③ Back fairly short, sloping slightly to rear

④ Tail short but not docked

⑤ Forelegs set wide, straight

❏ **Color:** any solid or partial color, but more than 80 percent white, black and tan, or liver are less preferred

❏ **DQ:** none

The American Staffordshire Terrier makes a devoted companion and protector.

The American Staffordshire Terrier is enormously powerful.

The early specimens—often called bull and terrier dogs or pit bull terriers—stemmed from bulldog and terrier crossings, with gameness the prime requirement. When dogfighting was outlawed, the breeding emphasis switched from ferocity to producing a dog extremely powerful for its size.

Over the years several different breeds developed from the early English stock: the American Staffordshire Terrier, the Staffordshire Bull Terrier, and the Bull Terrier. The breed was originally designated as the Staffordshire Terrier, with the name changed to its current one in 1972 to help distinguish it from the Staffordshire Bull Terrier. The American Staffordshire Terrier is known as the American Pit Bull Terrier in the United Kingdom, and there are some size differences between countries, with the American version being slightly taller and heavier.

Much has been written and said about the Pit Bull Terrier in recent days, and to many people this term designates a vicious fighting dog. The American Staffordshire Terrier suffers from this bad reputation. While a modern day American Staffordshire Terrier is still a courageous dog, viciousness is not a typical trait. Poorly trained animals that stem from aggressive dogs of mixed lineage are generally responsible for the atrocities attributed to "Pit Bull Terriers."

In appearance the breed is very powerfully built, with a short, sleek coat in any color but white that highlights its muscular body. It stands from 16 inches to 19 inches (40.7–

48.3 cm) in height and weighs approximately 45 to 60 pounds (20.4–27.2 kg). The ears can be either cropped or uncropped, and the tail is low set and not docked.

The American Staffordshire Terrier can be highly protective of its home and family, but is quite docile around the ones it loves. It does not care to share its home with another animal, but this and other game qualities can be moderated by obedience training, which is highly recommended. The breed is quite intelligent and takes well to such instruction. This dog wants to please its owners always and excels in police work and agility competition. Its grooming requirements are minimal; routine brushing and an occasional bath (as needed) will generally suffice.

This breed is not for everyone. It requires an experienced owner who can mold it into a loving companion by providing a substantial amount of vigorous exercise and competent obedience instruction.

Given adequate exercise, the American Staffordshire Terrier is normally a hardy breed, with an average life span of 10 to 12 years. There is a slight tendency toward hip and elbow dysplasia, and incidents of juvenile cataracts and immune system disorders have been noted. Litters average from five to ten puppies. Ear cropping is often performed by veterinarians when the puppies reach 12 weeks of age, but many fanciers are getting away from this.

Australian Terrier

Although developed in Australia during the 19th century, the Australian Terrier has close ties to many of the short-legged terriers that hail

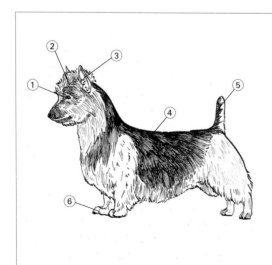

Illustrated Standard

1. Eyes small and oval
2. Head long and strong
3. Ears small, erect, and pointed
4. Topline level
5. Tail set high and carried at twelve o'clock, docked leaving just less than one half*
6. Small cat feet

❑ **Color:** blue and tan, solid sandy, and solid red
❑ **DQ:** none

*Docking is optional.

The Australian Terrier is very bright and relatively easy to keep looking presentable.

from the United Kingdom. As colonists made their way "down under," they brought various types of terriers with them. It is believed that the breed is a result of crossings of the native rough-coat terrier with imported Dandie Dinmont, Cairn, Manchester, Irish, Skye, and possibly Yorkshire Terrier strains.

Australian fanciers were most interested in producing a small, hardy terrier that could serve as a companion in the home as well as an adept worker and hunter. Because of the harsh climate, the dog had to possess a rugged, easy-to-care-for coat that could protect the dog from the environment as well as from predators. The Aus-

tralian excelled as a vermin and snake hunter, and was often used as guardian for the home and for live-stock herds in the bushland.

The Australian Terrier is one of the smallest of the working terriers, averaging about 10 inches (25.4 cm) in height and 12 to 14 pounds (5.4–6.3 kg) in weight, but its size does not prevent it from being one of the most energetic, outgoing terrier breeds. It is a very affectionate, personable dog that gets along well with everyone, including other dogs and housepets. The Australian is easygoing enough to be trusted around small children, yet game enough to serve as a reliable watch-dog. It is very alert to all events in its home environment and quick to sound an alarm when strangers approach. Despite this vivacious spirit, the breed is generally quiet and relaxed around the home, not exhibiting any sign of hyperactivity. It is a great companion for the elderly and is being used as a service dog for the handicapped.

This breed will thrive in any environment, in any size home, and needs only a moderate amount of exercise. The coat requires little more than a combing and brushing every few days to keep it looking neat. Shedding is minimal and bathing is needed infrequently. The long hairs that grow along the feet and ears, as well as any stray hairs in the coat, should be plucked for tidiness, but professional clipping is unnecessary. Inspect the skin frequently, however, since rashes can sometimes go unnoticed beneath the double coat; flea infestation can lead to serious irritations.

The Australian takes well to obedience training, which often helps to temper some of its exuberance. It is a very swift mover and should be kept on leash whenever outdoors to avoid a sudden dash into the path of danger.

Australian Terrier litters are often quite small, averaging only three or four puppies, which are born almost completely black. They develop their tan markings as they age. The tail is docked to two-fifths length. The Australian Terriers sport prick ears and a very keen expression.

The Aussie has a typical life span of 12 to 15 years. Incidences of dia-

Light and quick in its movements, the "Aussie" carries the heritage of his rough and tumble origins.

betes, Legg-Perthes disease (a hip disorder), and undescended testicles are found in the breed, although not common.

Bedlington Terrier

The Bedlington Terrier is often compared in appearance to a lamb, with its light "fluffy" coat, hanging ears, and a docile expression. Appearances can be deceiving. The Bedlington Terrier is a very game breed, a swift, powerful runner, and an eager hunter of small and mid-size game.

The breed was developed early in the 19th century in the village of

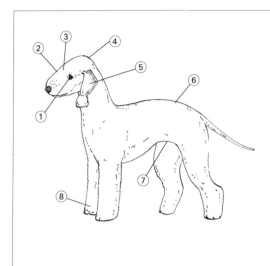

Illustrated Standard

1. Eyes almond shaped
2. Skull narrow, deep, and rounded
3. No stop
4. Profuse topknot
5. Ears triangular with rounded tips, hanging, set low, with a silky tassel at tip
6. Back has arch over loin
7. Good tuck-up
8. Hare feet

❏ **Color:** blue, sandy, and liver, each with or without tan points. Bedlington pups are born dark, and lighten to adult color by about one year of age.
❏ **DQ:** none

The Bedlington Terrier was used as a very capable hunter and an excellent racing dog.

Bedlington in Northumberland, England. The Bedlington is believed to have been derived from the Dandie Dinmont Terrier. Folklore has it that the Bedlingtons were used primarily by the gypsies of the Rothbury Forest, who trained the dogs to hunt the livestock of the rich landowners of the area. For a time, the breed was known as the Rothbury Terrier.

The Bedlington Terrier's high, arching back, attributed to crosses to sighthounds (probably Whippets) in the formative days of the breed, enables it to run with great speed and have good endurance. Your Bedlington needs ample opportunity to exercise and run, but also exhibits a tendency to bolt and chase any moving object when allowed off leash so be sure to have this terrier tethered when not in confined areas.

The Bedlington's lamblike exterior disguises its true, courageous nature.

The lamblike appearance of the Bedlington is not easily achieved, although it never goes "out of coat." The coat is nonshedding, comprised of a mixture of hard and soft hairs that stand out from the body. It takes regular, skillful trimming to get the desired look. The Bedlington Terrier coat has a color range from sandy to liver. Litters range in size from three to six puppies; the colors of the newborns generally lighten as the dogs mature.

While the Bedlington is generally quite hardy, it has shown tendencies toward eye problems. In the home, this terrier is a loyal, loving companion when not threatened by the presence of other animals. The Bedlington's inclination to jealousy makes it less suited to homes with small, active children than other more docile terrier breeds. A stubborn streak is best tempered from your dog's earliest days in the home by adequate obedience training. This will also lay the groundwork for the tolerance a Bedlington needs for the grooming regimen.

Black Russian Terrier

The Black Russian Terrier (BRT) is a new member of the Working Group, effective July 1, 2004, as the AKC's 151st recognized breed. It was developed in the 1930s by the Russian Central Military School of Working Dogs (also known as the Red Star Kennel), which bred dogs for guard work. Selective breedings

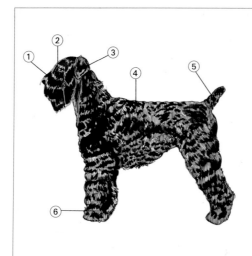

Illustrated Standard

(1) Powerful head
(2) Dark oval eyes
(3) High-set triangular ears, rather small
(4) Straight level topline
(5) Thick, high-set tail, docked to 3 to 5 vertebra
(6) Large round feet

❏ **Color:** black or black with a few gray hairs
❏ **DQ:** height under 26″; nose other than black; undershot or overshot bite; any color other than black

The Black Russian Terrier is the embodiment of power.

of Rottweilers, Giant Schnauzers, Airedales, and Russian Water Dogs, among others, were used to develop a large, strong, working terrier that could endure the harshness of the cold Russian climate.

Over the next seventy years the breed was stabilized, with the modern BRT being a robust, high-spirited dog that is eager to work and able to withstand the harshest climates. The breed continues to be used in police work and is described as having the ability of the German Shepherd Dog while being less aggressive. Males are more massive than the females, with weights ranging from 80 to more than 140 pounds (36.4–63.7 kg).

The Black Russian Terrier is suited for guard work because it is observant and suspicious of strangers, with a strong protective instinct. However, it does not function well as

The Black Russian Terrier was developed in the mid-20th century as a guard and police dog.

a kennel dog, as it requires close human contact. It is a family dog that gets along with children as well as other dogs and animals (although males do not do well in households with two dominant dogs).

A Black Russian Terrier puppy is very active and if left alone will get into everything. Obedience training should begin when young and housetraining should be relatively easy for this quick-to-learn breed.

The Black Russian Terrier does not have significant exercise requirements and can be kept in good trim if given long, daily walks. Given the opportunity, it will love a romp in the snow or a dash into nearby water. Despite its size, it is amenable to

apartment life if properly exercised, as it will remain relatively inactive indoors. In fact, if left alone in the yard "to play," it will probably quickly return to the door and sit quietly until let back into the house.

The BRT takes a long time to fully mature and its life expectancy is 10 to 11 years. The breed has a tendency toward hip dysplasia, as the early stock was not well monitored for this genetic tendency. However, over the last few decades dedicated breeders have focused on ridding this disorder from the breeding stock. Additionally, the ears must be well cared for to prevent otitis. Carefully removing hairs from the ear ducts is a helpful preventive measure.

The Border Terrier's head resembles that of an otter.

The breed's weatherproof coat is comprised of wiry, wavy hair, with a tight undercoat. Its eyebrows, beard, and mane are highlights. The BRT sheds very little if brushed at least once a week, but professional grooming is required two or three times a year.

Border Terrier

The Border Terrier evolved from various terrier strains that were found in the hill country of England in the area that *borders* Scotland. This hardy working terrier was unmatched in its ability to seek out and kill the predators of the local livestock, and it was admired for being able to subdue even the more vicious animals through a combination of courage, stamina, and cunning. The first Border Terrier registration in America was in 1930.

In appearance, the Border Terrier is often described as "plain." It

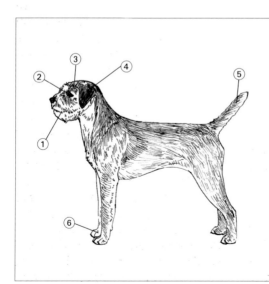

Illustrated Standard

① Muzzle short, darker colored and with a few short whiskers
② Eyes medium sized
③ Head similar to an otter
④ Small, V-shaped ears, dropping forward
⑤ Tail moderately short, carried gaily when alert
⑥ Feet small

❏ **Color:** red, grizzle and tan, blue and tan, or wheaten
❏ **DQ:** none

The Border Terrier is often used by mounted fox hunts.

stands approximately 12 to 13 inches (30.7–33.3 cm) in height, has a wiry double coat, an erect, undocked tail, and a head that is said to resemble an otter's. While it is one of the smaller terriers, it is very capable. It takes easily and naturally to the hunt, yet is a bit more even-tempered than many of the feisty terrier breeds.

In the home the Border Terrier is a well-mannered companion that makes little demand on its owners. In personality, the Border Terrier is often described as "pleasant," and these dogs affably get along with other animals, unlike many terriers. Its coat is almost maintenance-free and seldom requires more than an occasional brushing and some limited trimming to keep stray hairs neat. It does require some vigorous exercise each day, as it has a lot of energy despite its small frame. The Border Terrier is quite sensitive to what is going on around it at all times, so it is advisable to keep it on leash when out walking, as it may be inclined to bolt after any small animal that it spies in the distance.

One of the more docile terriers, the Border breed fits well into the home. It is happy to serve as companion in an apartment setting, yet adapts well to a more rugged environment that includes small children and other pets. Its strong will is easily tempered by obedience lessons, which the dog takes to quite readily.

The Border Terrier is generally a very healthy and long-lived breed. Patellar luxation is the only known hereditary disease specific to this

The Boston Terrier's short face and undershot jaw link it to Bulldog types.

breed (in about 7 percent), and retained testicles, cataracts, ear problems, and skin diseases have also been reported. There are usually no breeding or whelping difficulties, and litters commonly range in size from three to six. It is found in a number of colors (red, tan, wheaten), with newborns of various colors found in the same litter.

The Border Terrier is a fine example of the true terrier. It has not been extensively refined over the years and remains today much like the early representatives of the breed. It is unspoiled, unpampered, and uninhibited.

Boston Terrier

At the beginning of the 20th century, the Boston Terrier was the most popular purebred dog in America. It currently ranks around 16th among the 150 recognized breeds. It boasts an affectionate nature, a lively personality, and a sociable outlook. It relishes the role of housepet, as it loves the company of children, adults, and even other pets. It will thrive in any environment, from city apartment to the country. This terrier is very alert to everything that goes on around it and is a natural watchdog.

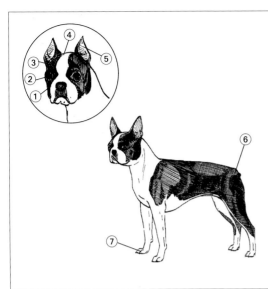

Illustrated Standard

1. Alert kind expression
2. Large, round eyes
3. Abrupt brow
4. Square, wrinkle-free skull
5. Small, erect ears, natural or cropped
6. Short straight or screw tail carried below level of back
7. Small round feet

❏ **Color:** brindle, seal, or black with white markings on muzzle, between eyes, and forechest, and possibly white collar and lower legs
❏ **DQ:** blue eyes, dudley nose, docked tail, liver or gray, lack of required white areas

The Boston Terrier is one of the few breeds actually developed in the United States, and its name attests to its homeland. It was originated by crossing terrier strains descended from the English Terrier with various types of bulldogs. Over the years it was slowly downgraded in size from an average of 35 pounds (15.9 kg) in the 19th century to its current weight of 15 to 25 pounds (6.8–11.3 kg). It averages about 17 inches (43.2 cm) in height and has a very short, square muzzle and large, round eyes. The preferred color is a brindle with white markings on the face, forehead, breast, and forelegs.

The Boston Terrier is assigned to the Nonsporting Group rather than the Terrier Group, as the breed was never intended as an earth dog; it lacks much of the game, aggressive nature typical of many of the terrier

Convenient size and ease of care are two of the Boston Terrier's many assets.

breeds. It does have a streak of stubbornness, however, that should be tempered by obedience training. Training the Boston Terrier to the rules of the household should be easily accomplished, as this is a very intelligent breed. It takes well to any type of home, and requires little more than a daily walk. An occasional grooming with a bristle brush or grooming glove is all that is needed to keep the coat smooth and shiny.

Because of its short muzzle, the Boston Terrier is often prone to respiratory ailments, and it may also snore and wheeze. Its eyes are easily injured and it is subject to skin ailments and tumors. The large head also often impedes normal delivery, so cesarean sections are common. Litters generally contain from three to five puppies, which become very active at a very early age and will need an early introduction to obedience training.

Bull Terrier

Many newcomers to this breed are surprised to discover that the Bull Terrier can be as gentle and loving as it is rugged looking. The breed's powerful build is highlighted by big-boned legs, muscular shoulders, and a well-rounded chest. The head is oval, with small, deeply set eyes that give the face a look of intelligence and confidence. There is also a Miniature Bull Terrier breed in the Terrier Group (see page 125).

The Bull Terrier was devised in 19th-century England primarily for

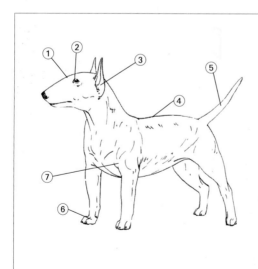

Illustrated Standard

① Head long, strong and deep, curving from skull to nose; oval outline viewed face on
② Eyes small, triangular, deep set, and placed close together
③ Ears small, erect, close set
④ Short strong back
⑤ Tail short, carried horizontally
⑥ Cat feet
⑦ Big boned but not coarse

❏ **Color:** white variety: white, with markings on head permissible; colored variety: any color other than white, or any color with white markings; brindle preferred
❏ **DQ:** blue eyes; in colored variety, any dog predominantly white

the purpose of dogfighting. Breeders crossed the bulldog of that time with a very game dog from the area called the English Terrier, to produce a dog with the strength and endurance of the former and the speed and punishing bite of the latter. Once dogfighting was abolished, the breed remained quite popular because of its unsurpassed loyalty to owner and home.

While it is obvious that the Bull Terrier is not the breed for everyone, it is very amiable, and people-oriented. It is a quick learner with very clean habits and mannerisms. The owner must be assertive with a Bull Terrier right from the start; more than elementary obedience training is required. With such guidance the Bull Terrier will mature into an excellent companion. The Bull Terrier does best in a single-pet household, as it is often not tolerant of other animals. It may also view any animal that enters its territory as an intruder. The Bull Terrier needs an outlet for its energy and will require at least one long walk daily. It loves all games with balls and craves companionship.

A twice weekly grooming with a hound glove or bristle brush is all that is needed to keep the Bull Terrier looking neat. Bathe these dogs only when necessary. All-white dogs naturally show dirt more than colored ones, and may require more cleanup if allowed much time outdoors.

The Bull Terrier usually weighs 50 to 60 pounds (22.7–27.2 kg) and stands approximately 22 inches (56

The Bull Terrier's courage is a hallmark of the breed. The Colored variety (illustrated) is older than the White.

Now familiar as an advertising icon, the Bull Terrier was bred to be a dauntless fighting dog.

cm) high. Its coat is short, glossy, and harsh to the touch, with various colors permissible. These include solid white, white with markings on the head, and brindled. Aside from a slight tendency for all-white Bull Terriers to have hearing problems, the breed is exceptionally hardy with an average life span of 10 to 12 years.

Incidences of zinc deficiency have been noted, which leads to death in afflicted puppies. An overabundance of testosterone is sometimes found in males, which leads to overaggressive behavior and territorial instinct. This is cured by neutering. Some Bull Terriers are also compulsive tail chasers, which can be controlled by medication. Litters typically contain four to eight puppies, with a variety of colors possible in every litter. No whelping problems are common.

Cairn Terrier

The Cairn is thought to be one of the oldest terrier breeds, dating back hundreds of years to its homeland on Britain's Isle of Skye. This terrier's task was always to hunt out the predators that stalked and hid in the "cairns" or rock piles of this area's rugged terrain. This was a job requiring skill, nimbleness, stamina, and a superior terrier gameness, and the Cairn Terrier earned a reputation for steadfastness against any obstacle.

The Cairn Terrier also earned high praise as a companion in the home, for it blended a strong sense of loyalty with a wariness of strangers, making it a natural watchman over home and children. The Cairn is very affectionate toward its loved ones, and is more outgoing and good-natured than many other terriers who

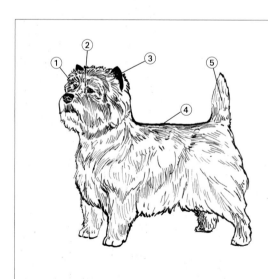

Illustrated Standard

① Eyes sunken, with shaggy eyebrows
② Skull broad, well-defined stop
③ Ears small, pointed, erect, set wide
④ Level back of medium length
⑤ Tail carried gaily but not curled over back

❑ **Color:** any color but white; dark ears, muzzle, tail tip desired
❑ **DQ:** none

The Cairn Terrier is a most personable breed and may be any solid color other than white.

sometimes become snappy when subjected to the roughhousing of children. Cairns take such tumult in stride and can often outlast the seemingly endless energy of children.

A Cairn Terrier goes about anything it undertakes with zeal. It is a very rugged and hardy breed, often living well into the teens. Its hard, weather-resistant coat requires only a moderate amount of grooming and no clipping to keep it tidy. Its exercise requirements are not excessive, but it does enjoy as much activity as it can have. Left alone in a yard it will amuse itself with digging, so gardeners beware! This does not, however,

The Cairn Terrier comes from the Scottish Highlands and the Isle of Skye. The breed has existed for centuries.

The Cesky Terrier was developed in Czechoslovakia following World War II. Ceskys are valiant earth dogs.

mean that the Cairn is not suited for a sedate household. This terrier gets along well in almost every situation, matching its daily activities to its master's schedule and interests. A Cairn will generally get along well with its own kind but often acts aggressively around other dogs.

A rare, ultimately fatal, genetic disease known as globoid cell leukodystrophy is present in some Cairn Terrier lines. This is a recessive disease that affects the brain. It can be carried by dogs not manifesting the disease, so it is important that all Cairn sires and dams be tested for this mutation before breeding.

Litters average three to five puppies, which can be any color but white. They housetrain easily. Cairns are very intelligent and can become a bit devious if allowed to rule their home without restrictions, so basic obedience training is suggested.

Like almost every true terrier, the Cairn will follow its instincts and bolt after any small animal that appears, so be sure to keep the dog on leash when not in a fenced lot.

The Cairn is one of the most cherished house pets among the terrier breeds. Its personality is all but faultless: pleasant, loving, happy, devoted. There is a lot of dog in this small frame.

Cesky Terrier

The Cesky (ches-kee) Terrier, also known as the Czesky or Bohemian Terrier, was developed in Czechoslovakia in the late 1940s by geneticist Frantisek Horak, who wanted a dog small enough to go to ground and hunt small vermin. He believed the local breeds had become too broad in the chest, so he selected

Cesky Terrier.

the Scottish and the Sealyham Terriers for his early breedings. These dogs imparted his hunting dogs with longer legs, narrower chests, and a smaller head than the local breeds. By 1960 the breed type was set, but exportations were very limited. The breed slowly spread throughout Europe over the next twenty years. The first Ceskys were imported to the United States in the 1980s, but the breed still remains relatively rare. While the Cesky Terrier has not gained formal breed recognition by the American Kennel Club, it was approved for competition in AKC earth dog tests as of January 1, 2004.

The Cesky Terrier is still revered as a national breed in Czechoslovakia, where it has been featured on a postage stamp. It is still used widely for hunting rabbits, fox, birds, and the occasional wild boar.

The Cesky Terrier is of medium length, weighs 13 to 22 pounds (5.9–9.9 kg) (with the ideal weight being 16 to 20 pounds [7.2–9.1 kg]), stands 10 to 12 inches (25–30 cm) at the shoulders, and has an undocked tail 78 inches (195 cm) in length.

The Cesky coat is nonshedding and is kept trim by electric clippers; it should not be stripped like most other terriers. It should be combed and brushed twice a week to prevent matting. Clipping is needed every 10 to 12 weeks to keep the dog looking tidy. The coat is soft and not wiry and is either gray (with many shadings) or light brown, but gray is most common. Some white is permissible on the chest, feet, and neck. Puppies are born black or dark brown and it can take up to two years for the coat to fully lighten.

The Cesky Terrier is less aggressive than the Scottie and Sealyham,

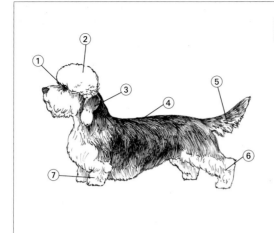

Illustrated Standard

① Large, round eyes
② Head is covered with soft silky hair
③ Ears set low, hanging
④ Topline is low at withers, arching over the loin
⑤ Tail is long, carried a little above the level of the body, with a curve
⑥ Hindlegs slightly longer than forelegs
⑦ Round feet

❏ **Color:** pepper (all shades of gray and silver) or mustard (all shades of brown and fawn). Dandie Dinmont puppies are much darker than adults.
❏ **DQ:** none

and it gets along well with other dogs. It is a natural housepet, extremely loyal to and protective of its family. Initially reserved with strangers, it quickly warms to new people after being introduced and is naturally friendly with children. This breed is a quick learner and takes well to obedience training.

The life span of the Cesky Terrier is approximately 12 to 15 years. A moderate amount of exercise is all that is needed to keep the Cesky from getting bored and out of trim, but this dog is happy to be treated as a lapdog. The breed is robust and generally has few health problems. Incidences have been reported of the genetic disorder known as "Scottie cramp," which impacts walking ability in situations of extreme stress or excitement. This is not life threaten-ing and usually subsides as soon as the dog quiets down.

Dandie Dinmont Terrier

The Dandie Dinmont Terrier is a "Scotch" type of terrier. It is very short in the leg and long in the body, but has pendulous ears—a trait that came late to the terriers of Scotland. The breed is thought to be related to the other terriers that hail from this area of the British Isles, the Border and Bedlington Terriers.

The breed attracted much attention with the publication in 1814 of *Guy Mannering,* by Sir Walter Scott. In this novel a character named Dandie Dinmont had six feisty terriers of pepper and mustard coloring that

The Dandie Dinmont Terrier's curved body differs from the sharp angles usually associated with most other terrier breeds.

excelled not only as vermin hunters but as intelligent, loyal companions. The breed traces its name to this fictional character, who did much to popularize a breed that had previously been confined to the wilds of Scotland.

The Dandie Dinmont Terrier is a very game dog, prone to challenging other animals—whether a predatory fox or another dog (especially males). If this tendency is not tempered from youth, the Dandie will be unruly around other animals as an adult. Obedience training is a must, as is a leash at all times when the dog is outdoors. It is often an extraordinary digger. The Dandie can be

The Dandie Dinmont Terrier is the only dog breed named for a fictional character. Sir Walter Scott gave the breed its name in 1814.

quite stubborn, so be patient and firm if it should rebel.

The typical height for a Dandie Dinmont is 8 to 11 inches (20.3–28.0 cm) at the top of the shoulder, and it weighs from 18 to 24 pounds (8.2–10.9 kg). Litters generally contain three to six puppies, and maturity comes late to the breed. The adult coat color will normally be set by about eight months of age, but it will take two to three years for the dog to reach physical maturity.

The Dandie Dinmont is a hardy breed that can withstand a rigorous lifestyle with no apparent stress, although having to climb stairs may cause back problems for susceptible dogs. The coat is about 2 inches (5.1 cm) in length, with a mixture of hard and soft hairs. Grooming requirements are moderate, as it sheds little, but a brushing every other day is recommended to keep the hair from matting. Keeping the typical Dandie look is best handled by a professional. A moderate amount of exercise is advisable, but the Dandie can be kept in an urban setting without problem.

The Dandie Dinmont is a sensible housepet. It learns household manners fairly quickly and is quite intelligent, paying close attention to what goes on around it. Its loyalty is intense. Should the circumstances arise, a Dandie Dinmont might not take well to a new home once original attachments have been made.

Fox Terrier (Smooth and Wire)

The Smooth and Wire Fox Terriers date back to the mid-1800s; they were developed by hunt masters who required the services of a game, compact dog to flush the fox once it had gone to earth. The two breeds are now accepted by the American Kennel Club as distinct breeds, with the only true difference being the coat. The Toy Fox Terrier (see page 112) was developed in the 1920s

The Smooth Fox Terrier is the traditional companion of the mounted hunt, but is also a familiar figure in circus dog acts.

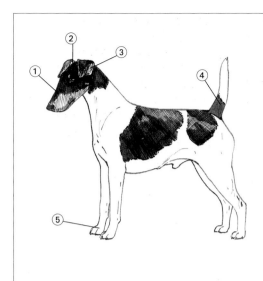

Illustrated Standard

1. Skull flat and moderately narrow, head 7–7.25″ long
2. Rather small, deep-set, round eyes
3. Small, V-shaped ears, dropping forward with fold above skull level
4. Tail set high and carried gaily, but not over back or curled; about one fourth docked off
5. Feet round and compact

❏ **Color:** white should predominate (brindle, red, or liver markings are objectionable)
❏ **DQ:** ears prick, tulip, or rose; nose white, cherry or considerably spotted with white or cherry; much undershot or overshot

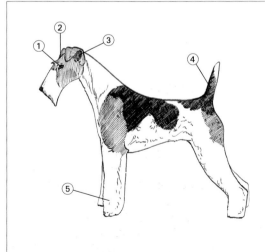

Illustrated Standard

1. Rather small, deep-set, and round eyes
2. Skull flat and moderately narrow, head 7–7.25″ long
3. Small, V-shaped ears, dropping forward with fold above skull level
4. Tail set high and carried gaily, but not over back or curled; about one fourth docked off
5. Feet round and compact

❏ **Color:** white should predominate (brindle, red, or liver markings are objectionable)
❏ **DQ:** ears prick, tulip, or rose; nose white, cherry or considerably spotted with white or cherry; much undershot or overshot

The Wire Fox Terrier is a capable earth dog and one of the world's most successful show dogs.

master any number of tricks and has often been used as a circus performer. It is an energetic dog that enjoys an active lifestyle. While the breed can do well with elderly or sedentary owners, it does best with those who can put it through its paces, such as a family with children.

The Smooth Fox Terrier requires little more than an occasional brushing with a hound glove or bristle brush to keep the coat shiny and healthy. The Wire Fox Terrier requires more attention. A show dog will need to have its coat regularly stripped and plucked to maintain proper texture and tidiness. A pet Wire Fox Terrier may be clipped to maintain a neat appearance, but this will somewhat soften the coat from the ideal texture described in the breed standard; this does not, however, present any health risks.

Fox Terriers are hardy dogs but can be subject to skin problems. They are often allergic to flea bites, which result in rashes and dermatitis. This is usually easily cured by keeping the environment clean and using topical ointments and chemical repellents. Wire and Smooth bitches generally have few whelping difficulties; their litters usually contain from three to six puppies.

from selective breedings of small Smooth Fox Terrier specimens.

The Fox Terrier averages from 16 to 18 pounds (7.3–8.2 kg) and stands up to 15½ inches (39.4 cm) at the withers. All sport a muscular, well-contoured body.

The Fox Terrier is a people-oriented dog that makes a welcome housepet. It is friendly and personable, with a desire to get in on all the happenings of the family rather than watch from the sidelines. Regardless of type or size, the Fox Terrier is a natural watchdog, and even may go a bit too far by being overly vocal (let's face it, they bark a lot). With a little training, the Fox Terrier can

Fox Terrier (Toy)

The Toy Fox Terrier was recognized as the American Kennel Club's 148th breed and is a member of the Toy Group. Also known as the

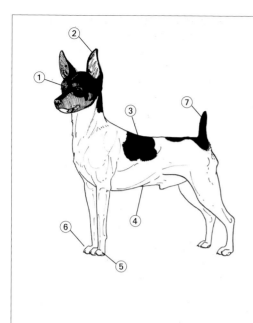

Illustrated Standard

① Round, somewhat prominent eyes
② Erect, pointed, high-set ears
③ Level topline
④ Moderate tuck-up
⑤ Straight pasterns
⑥ Small oval feet
⑦ High-set tail, held erect, docked to third or fourth vertebra

❏ **Color:** tri-color; white, chocolate and tan; white and tan; or white and black, all with predominately colored head and more than 50% white on body

❏ **DQ:** under 8.5″ or over 11.5″; ears not erect on dog over six months old; dudley nose; undershot, wry mouth, or overshot more than 1/8″; blaze extending into eye or ears; any but stated color combinations; more than 50% white on head; less than 50% white on body

The Toy Fox Terrier has been a popular pet for many years and gained AKC recognition on January 1, 2003.

113

A Toy Fox Terrier is as spunky as its larger terrier buddies.

American Toy Terrier or Amertoy, the breed type was set in the United States in the 1930s by pairing the Smooth Fox Terrier with toys, including the Chihuahua, Italian Greyhound, and Toy Manchester Terrier. The result was a dog diminutive in size only, with the spunky spirit of a terrier and the mild disposition of a lapdog. While primarily a companion, the Toy Fox Terrier still delights in chasing squirrels and flushing out any rodent that may enter its terrain.

This breed's energy is endless. It loves to fetch and will be willing to do so long after the human at the other end of the ball has given up. Most of its exercise requirements are easily met from its daily patrol of the household, as it is a fearless watchdog that is alert to unusual situations while barking only when necessary. Despite its size, the Toy Fox has shown an uncanny ability in flyball, obedience, and agility competition. It has also been trained for work as a hearing dog for the deaf and to provide other in-home aid to handicapped owners.

While generally a very hearty breed, with a 13- to 14-year life span, the Toy Fox Terrier is quite small and can suffer broken bones if stepped on or involved in a major fall. This also makes the breed unsuitable around very small children, who may treat it too roughly. Owners should be on the lookout for allergic reactions to dry food, as this breed has shown an intolerance for several of the common additives in kibble. The major genetic health concern involves leg problems, which will become noticeable while the dog is young, if present.

Grooming the Toy Fox Terrier involves little more than an occasional brushing to remove stray hairs and keeping the nails trimmed. It doesn't tolerate the cold well and should be dressed in a sweater if taken out when the temperature plunges.

Because of its size, the Toy Fox Terrier bitch can be prone to whelping problems. Litters usually contain only two or three puppies.

Glen of Imaal Terrier

The Glen of Imaal Terrier is named for the small, secluded valley in southeast Ireland of the same name. Life in this beautiful but infertile glen in County Wicklow was difficult and most residents were subsistence farmers. (In fact, this land was so unforgiving that it was abandoned in the early 1900s and turned into an artillery range that is still in use today by the Irish Army.) This low-to-the-ground, powerful terrier was initially bred to rid the home and farm of vermin and go down into an animal's den and drag it out. It is believed that the early Glens were also used as "turnspit" dogs—trotting on a treadmill to turn cooking meats. Their bowed front legs and powerful hindquarters were good for this.

The Glen is believed to be indigenous to that secluded area of Ireland, having evolved over the centuries from local stock. There is no direct evidence that any interbreeding took place with its Irish cousins (the Kerry Blue, Irish, or Soft Coated Wheaten Terriers and the Irish Wolfhound). There are documented reports of the Glen at Irish dog shows as early as 1878, but recognition by the Irish Kennel Club didn't come until 1934. The breed traveled to Great Britain and later the United States, but the numbers were small until the late 1980s. The Glen was accepted into the AKC's Miscellaneous Class on September 1, 2001, and was moved into the Terrier Group as of October 1, 2004. It is also a regular competitor in obedience, agility, and earth dog competition.

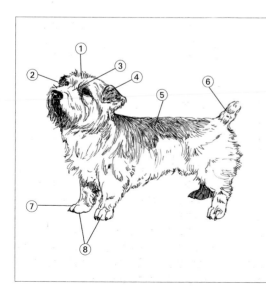

Illustrated Standard

1. Powerful head
2. Round eyes
3. Pronounced stop
4. Rose or half-prick ears
5. Topline straight, slightly rising to loin
6. Tail docked to about half length, carried gaily
7. Forelegs short, bowed, and well-boned
8. Forefeet turned out slightly

❏ **Color:** wheaten, blue, or brindle

The Glen of Imaal Terrier was recognized by the AKC on October 1, 2004, and is the fourth of the terriers of Ireland to join the Terrier Group in the United States.

The Glen of Imaal Terrier is the epitome of the terrier reputation of gameness: plucky, hardy, with an unyielding spirit. There are two say-

The Glen of Imaal's head is strikingly similar to that of the Irish Wolfhound.

ings that aptly fit this breed: "It's a big dog on short legs" and "It won't start a fight, but it will likely finish one." Owners should be aware that the Glen can be aggressive with other dogs that it is not familiar with, but it can live amicably with those it is raised with (and usually cats as well).

In the home a Glen is an inquisitive, loving companion for both adults and children. However, its strength belies its size and a child should not be allowed to hold this dog on a leash. While there is a distinct streak of independence and stubbornness, the Glen responds eagerly to praise and sensitively to a scolding. It is a natural watchdog that was bred to work silently, so it only barks when provoked, but when it does the tone is so deep that it sounds like a much larger dog. It is not hyper and its exercise requirements are easily met with a long walk—although it will never turn down a run in the woods.

The Glen of Imaal breed is generally robust, with a life expectancy of from 12 to 14 years. There is a genetic tendency toward hip dysplasia and progressive retinal atrophy (PRA), an inherited eye disease that causes blindness. PRA usually does not become apparent until age two or later, so an annual test should be performed to rule this out. Hip dysplasia can be ruled out by X rays at the age of two.

The Glen's harsh coat sheds little, but it will mat if left unbrushed. The coat should be stripped twice a year, along with a thorough brushing with a slicker brush at least once a week.

Irish Terrier

This breed dates back at least to the 17th century to the homes of Irish laborers, who used their dogs to rid the fields of small predators. The Irish Terrier proved itself an all-around worker, eagerly turning to any task its master required of it—whether guarding the home, flushing a fox, or being a sporting companion.

This dog typifies the legendary terrier courage, but intense gameness is easily tempered by early training and the result is a superb housepet. It will thrive in any environment, in any size home, but requires some additional daily exercise beyond what is gained in the normal course of an active terrier's day. The Irish Terrier is not much for relaxation, and prefers to keep itself busy by investigating its surround-

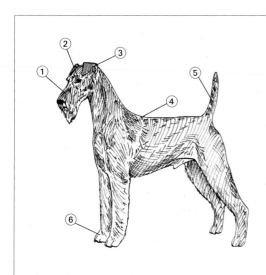

Illustrated Standard

① Head long and fairly narrow
② Eyes small, with intense expression
③ Small, V-shaped ears, dropping forward with fold above skull level
④ Body moderately long
⑤ Tail set high but not curled; about one fourth docked off
⑥ Feet rounded

❑ **Color:** red, golden red, red wheaten, or wheaten
❑ **DQ:** none

The Irish Terrier is generally lighter-bodied and longer than other similar terrier breeds.

ings for any new object of interest. It takes eagerly to the attention of children and can be trusted to be sensi-

Nicknamed the "daredevil," the Irish Terrier is one of the most fearless of all dogs.

ble in its reaction to unintentional rough treatment. While tolerant of humans, the Irish Terrier rarely gets along well with adult dogs of the same sex, so it does best in a one-dog home.

The Irish Terrier is moderately sized, averaging 18 inches (46 cm) in height and weighing 25 to 27 pounds (11.3–12.2 kg). It has a long, narrow head with small, V-shaped ears and expressive eyes. The coat is dense and wiry and requires only routine brushing and combing. It varies in color from bright red to wheaten, and any scraggly hairs are easily removed by plucking.

Loyal to the extreme, the Irish Terrier is a natural watchdog. It is quick to investigate all unusual noises and inspects all visitors to the household. If the need should arise, this dog would immediately come to the defense of its masters. This instinct for the fight will also quickly surface when male meets male.

The Irish Terrier is a hardy dog with few health or whelping problems. A small number of this breed suffer from hypothyroidism and cataracts. The average life span is 10 to 13 years. Litters generally contain four to seven puppies. The young may have a darker coat due to some black hairs that will disappear as the dogs mature.

Kerry Blue Terrier

This lighthearted breed takes its name from the County Kerry area of Ireland, where this terrier has long been used as a working, hunting, and companion dog. It dates back to the 1800s and was owned primarily by County Kerry farmers, who valued the breed's feisty temperament and mischievous nature.

It is one of the larger terriers, averaging around 18 to 19 inches (46.0–48.2 cm) at the withers and up to 40 pounds (18.1 kg) in weight. It is muscular and well balanced, with small, V-shaped ears and an erectly carried docked tail. It is every bit the terrier, from its solid conformation and angular profile to its spunky personality.

The Kerry Blue's distinctive blue-gray coat is the hallmark of the breed. It is a soft, dense coat that sheds very little and seldom gives off an offensive odor. There is no downy undercoat that is typically found in most terrier breeds. The coat is not

without grooming requirements, however. It must be regularly and thoroughly brushed and combed (daily is best), and needs scissor clipping every few months. The necessary trimming can be mastered with proper instruction and lots of practice; however, some owners may prefer to leave this task to a professional groomer.

This breed is generally very robust and can be long-lived, with an average life span of 12 to 15 years. There is a slight tendency toward eye problems (cataracts and tear deficiency). Kerry Blue litters generally contain five to eight puppies, and they will appear nearly black at birth. It takes 18 months or more for the final coat color to stabilize.

The Kerry Blue Terrier's coat and color are distinctive among all breeds.

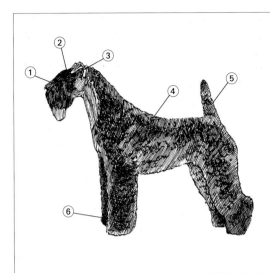

Illustrated Standard

1. Head long
2. Eyes small, keen expression
3. Small, V-shaped ears, dropping forward with fold above skull level
4. Back short and straight
5. Tail set high, carried gaily erect and straight
6. Feet fairly round and moderately small

❏ **Color:** any shade of blue-gray in mature (over 18 months) dog; immature dogs may be very dark blue or have tinges of brown

❏ **DQ:** solid black, dewclaws on hind legs

The Kerry Blue Terrier evolved in southern Ireland as a working dog. Wonderful guards and companions, Kerries are also excellent hunters and retain their ability to herd livestock.

The Kerry Blue is very personable and enjoys the company of humans more than that of other dogs. It can be an aggressive breed and it will never back down from a challenge or a fight with another dog; this is particularly prevalent when male meets male. The owner of a Kerry Blue Terrier must be a firm disciplinarian, as this breed is extremely determined and strong-willed. Obedience training is a must; be prepared for some confrontations during the early lessons. Once the dog accepts a master, however, it can learn quickly and efficiently. Kerry Blues have done very well in obedience competition.

While the Kerry Blue does not require extensive exercise, it is recommended that the dog be allowed a spirited run at regular intervals. The breed does best in a home with a yard, rather than in an apartment. It is a natural watchdog and will devotedly protect its loved ones. The Kerry Blue is at its best when surrounded by people and will often create little games to amuse those around it. It is jovial, fun-loving, and above all enthusiastic.

Lakeland Terrier

The Lakeland Terrier originated in the mountainous northwestern section of England from matings of the native terrier strains with what are thought to be the early Dandie Dinmont, Bedlington, and Border Terrier specimens. It was originally called the Patterdale Terrier. The breed was used primarily to keep the area clear of the foxes that preyed on the livestock. This was a dangerous task that required unmatched courage and stamina in a dog with a small, compact body that could squeeze into the foxes' burrows. Lakelands, generally used with teams of hounds during the hunt, were called on to flush the foxes once they went underground. The breed excelled at its work and would willingly dig into a predator's lair to accomplish the assigned task.

The Lakeland Terrier is not found in great numbers in the United States, but this is not a consequence of its personality. It is very personable and enjoys the company of both

Though relatively small in numbers, Lakeland Terriers have triumphed at some of America's most important shows.

The Lakeland Terrier is a superb earth dog and can squeeze into the narrowest crevices in pursuit of small game.

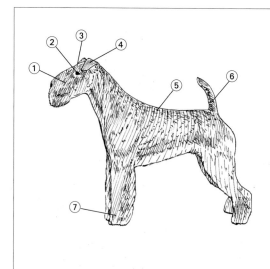

Illustrated Standard

1. Head appears rectangular from all angles
2. Eyes moderately small and oval
3. Stop barely perceptible
4. Small, V-shaped ears, dropping forward with fold above skull level
5. Topline short and level
6. Tail set high, carried upright with a slight curve forward; docked to about same height as occiput
7. Feet round

❑ **Color:** solid (blue, black, liver, red, or wheaten); or wheaten or golden tan with a saddle of blue, black, liver or grizzle
❑ **DQ:** teeth overshot or undershot

adults and children. It is a natural watchdog, and is quick to give voice if any noise or movement seems out of place. Like all terriers, the Lakeland is a game, highly energetic breed; this should always be considered by potential owners. It enjoys an active life, and does not take well to the presence of other animals; this is especially true of males.

The dog stands 14 to 15 inches (36.0–38.1 cm) in height and weighs approximately 17 pounds (7.7 kg). It has a rectangular head, small, V-shaped ears, and an intense expression that reveals the dog's self-confidence.

The coat of the Lakeland Terrier is two-ply, with a hard outer coat and a soft undercoat. It requires regular brushing and trimming. To maintain the desired texture, you will need to strip or pluck the outer coat two or three times a year. Nonshow dogs can have the coat clipped to an easily manageable length.

The Lakeland is usually very robust, exhibiting no predominant health problems. While the average life span is 12 to 13 years, many live as long as 16. It requires more exercise than one would suspect for a dog of this size. Litters usually contain from three to six puppies, and a puppy's coat will not reach the proper texture and color until maturity.

Manchester Terrier (Standard and Toy)

The Manchester Terrier is one of the oldest terrier breeds, tracing its ancestry back as far as the 1500s.

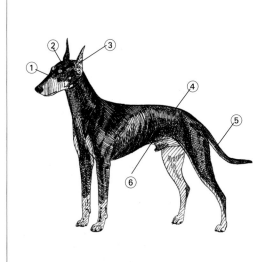

Illustrated Standard

① Head resembles a blunted wedge in profile and from front
② Small, almond-shaped eyes
③ Naturally erect, button, or cropped ear
④ Slight arch over loin
⑤ Tapered tail carried in a slight upward curve
⑥ Tucked up abdomen

❏ **Color:** black and tan, with a black "thumbprint" patch on the front of each foreleg and "pencil marks" on the top of each toe
❏ **DQ:** patch of white over 1/2 inch at its longest dimension, any color other than black and tan, weight over 22 lb. (in Toy variety only: cropped or cut ears)

The most obvious differences between the Toy Manchester Terrier (shown) and the Standard variety is size and the requirement for naturally erect ears in the Toy.

This Standard Manchester Terrier has cropped ears, but in this variety ears can also be naturally erect or "button" or folded.

These dogs were highly valued for their usefulness as rat catchers; pound for pound they had no match when it came to courage and native smartness. Over the years crosses to sighthounds, probably whippets, helped rid the breed of its coarseness and to give it extra speed for hunting rabbits. The breed was originally known as the black-and-tan terrier or the "gentleman's terrier," but it flourished in the Manchester section of England and was officially given this town's name in the 1920s.

This breed is found in two sizes. The Standard variety Manchester Terrier weighs from 12 to 22 pounds (5.4–10 kg), while the Toy variety (which is placed in the Toy Group) weighs less than 12 pounds (5.4 kg). Many Toy Manchesters are 5 pounds and less. Maximum and minimum heights are not listed in the breed standard, but Standard variety Manchesters are generally 15 to 16 inches (38.1–41.0 cm) tall, while the Toys are 11 inches (28 cm) or smaller.

The Manchester Terrier's coat is jet black with mahogany markings. It is smooth, dense, and exceptionally glossy. Grooming requirements are minimal. An occasional brushing with a bristle brush is enough to keep the coat in fine shape. It is a very hardy breed with few notable health problems, although a rare specimen may show signs of Legg-Perthes disease (a hip problem), von Willebrand's disease (a blood disorder), and hypothyroidism. Litters generally range from two to four puppies.

In the home the Manchester Terrier is a fine pet for all ages. Care should be taken, however, to teach children how to play with the Toy variety; with such limited size comes restrictions on roughhousing. The Manchester is naturally clean, intelligent, and well-behaved, and will adapt to any surroundings. The Manchester Terrier enjoys exercise and frequent walks with its owners and makes its pleasure known by being a very affectionate companion. It is particularly attuned to what is going on around it and sensitive to its loved ones' feelings and moods. While the Manchester Terrier is one of the least outwardly aggressive terrier breeds, it still does best when the sole dog in the house.

Miniature Bull Terrier

The Miniature Bull Terrier joined the American Kennel Club's Terrier Group in 1991 as the 133rd breed, but the breed dates back to England in the 1800s. The Bulldog and the now-extinct White English Terrier played the major role in fashioning the "bull and terrier" now known as the Bull Terrier. The Spanish Pointer is also mentioned as a distant ancestor.

From the beginning, size varied greatly in the offspring, and by the 1930s the dogs were broken into two breeds, based strictly on size. The Miniature Bull Terrier was limited to 14 inches (33 cm) in height

The Miniature Bull Terrier is every bit as courageous as his larger cousin.

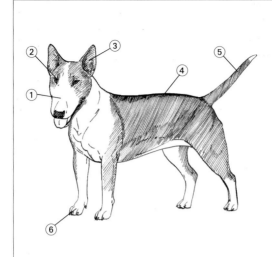

Illustrated Standard

1. Long, strong, deep head, curving from skull to nose; oval outline viewed face on
2. Eyes small, triangular, deep set, and placed close together
3. Ears small, erect, close set
4. Short strong back, slight arch over loin
5. Tail short, carried horizontally
6. Cat feet

❏ **Color:** for white: pure white; for colored: any color to predominate
❏ **DQ:** none

The Miniature Bull Terrier enjoyed an enthusiastic following in England before the breed was recognized by AKC in 1991.

and up to 33 pounds (15 kg), while the full-sized Bull Terrier goes to 22 inches (56 cm) and can weigh up to 60 pounds (27 kg). The Miniature is every bit as strong and muscular pound for pound as its larger relative, with a square, powerful look. The breed's triangular eyes and erect ears on its oval head are distinctive.

The Miniature Bull Terrier is full of life and often called a clown. Always ready for fun, the Miniature is great with children and takes well to life in a house or apartment as long as given time outdoors several times a day. It will get along well with most other dogs, but it must be socialized while young to accept cats, if you want them in the home together.

Devoted to owner and home, the breed is a natural watchdog that will sound an alarm at anything unusual (while not being prone to bark easily). This cheerful disposition is balanced with a courageous and amenable spirit. The breed takes well to instruction, and early socialization to new places, people, and things—as well as the rules of the house—will keep any innate desire to dominate in check.

Overall, the breed is quite healthy, with an average life span of 12 to 13 years. There are instances of deafness, especially in white specimens. A small number of puppies develop a zinc deficiency, which can cause death; this is thought to be genetically linked and does not appear in most breeding stock. Like the larger Bull Terrier, the Miniature sometimes develops a compulsive behavior, such as "spinning," where it constantly chases its tail. If this becomes a problem, medication may be in order. There can also be instances of overzealous territoriality, which is often cured by neutering. The Bull Terrier can also be a notorious chewer, especially when young or when left alone too long, and will quickly rip apart most any object left lying around, so it is necessary to have a supply of indestructible chew toys on hand at all times.

Norfolk and Norwich Terriers

While the Norfolk and Norwich Terriers stand only 10 inches (25.4 cm) in height and weigh a mere 11 to 12 pounds (5.0–5.4 kg), they are

Norfolk Terriers are equally adaptable to life in any environment.

every ounce the terrier. These breeds date from the early 1800s in the Norwich section of England. The Norwich, and its sister breed the Norfolk, were fostered by the country farmers to help clear the fields of small predators. These terriers were valued for their courage, stamina, and ease of care. Their harsh double coat was weather-resistant and trouble-free, and these dogs proved themselves tireless workers, willing to dig into any furrow in search of game. This trait also led to their popularity as a hunting companion for the gentry, who would use them to flush the fox that went underground during the hunt. The tail of the Norfolk and Norwich has traditionally

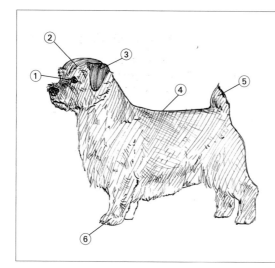

Illustrated Standard

1. Small, oval eyes
2. Skull wide, slightly rounded
3. V-shaped ears, tips slightly rounded, dropped with a break at skull level
4. Topline level
5. Tail medium docked, set on high
6. Feet round

❏ **Color:** all shades of red, wheaten, black and tan, or grizzle
❏ **DQ:** none

been docked to a medium length so that it could be grasped to help extricate the dog, if, in its feisty determination, it dug itself in too deeply during a chase.

For many years the Norfolk and Norwich Terriers were regarded as two varieties within the same breed, differentiated mainly by their ear set.

In 1979 the breeds were separated by the American Kennel Club, following the action taken in England by the Kennel Club in 1964. The Norfolk has small, dropped ears, while the Norwich has medium-sized, erect ears. The two breeds also differ in body proportion, with the Norfolk's length of the back

Highly sociable, Norfolk Terriers tend to enjoy each other's company.

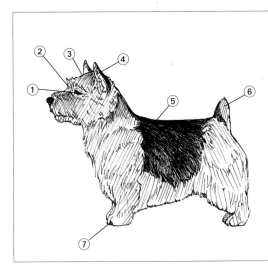

1. Small, oval eyes
2. Well-defined stop
3. Skull broad and slightly rounded
4. Medium-sized ears, erect with pointed tips
5. Topline level
6. Tail medium docked, carried erect
7. Feet round

❏ **Color:** all shades of red, wheaten, black and tan, or grizzle
❏ **DQ:** none

The Norwich Terrier is distinguished from the Norfolk by its erect ears and more compact body.

A Norwich Terrier is not difficult to keep in shape; most owners acquire the required skill easily.

being slightly longer than its height at the withers while the Norwich's is approximately equal.

Today's Norfolk and Norwich Terriers are ideal companions for all. Their exercise requirements are moderate, yet they can participate in the most vigorous of activities. Always bear in mind that these breeds were originally working terriers and still exhibit many of the traits that served the early specimens of the breed so well. The most troublesome trait is the desire to dig. These little terriers can do quite a bit of damage to a garden—especially if

they spot a rabbit running for cover. The Norfolk and Norwich can also be escape artists, so set fences deeply to prevent these dogs from digging their way to freedom. Another inborn tendency is to chase after all small animals, so keep these dogs on leash whenever not in a confined location.

The personable Norfolk and Norwich Terriers thrive on attention and can get along with young and old. They are trustworthy around children, and intensely loyal. If startled or threatened, they can be relied upon to react with restraint. Such self-control is sometimes lacking in other terrier breeds. They also distinguish themselves from other terriers by living rather peacefully with other household pets. They are natural watchdogs and will maintain a constant eye on the goings on around them, giving ample voice in the event of any strange sound or occurrence.

The Norfolk and Norwich are healthy breeds and often quite long-lived with an expected life span of 12 to 15 years. A rare genetic problem is epilepsy. There are generally no whelping problems, and litters usually contain three or four puppies.

Parson Russell Terrier

As legend has it, the Parson Russell Terrier (also known as the Parson Jack Russell Terrier or just Jack Russell Terrier) was developed in the

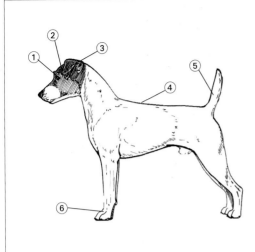

Illustrated Standard

① Almond-shaped eyes
② Skull flat
③ Button ears; small V-shaped drop ear carried forward with the tip pointing toward the eye
④ Topline straight, with loin slightly arched
⑤ Tail set high and carried gaily; docked so tip is about level with skull
⑥ Cat feet

❏ **Color:** predominantly white with tan, black, or brown markings
❏ **DQ:** under 12″ or over 15″ tall; prick ears; liver nose; four or more missing teeth; overshot, undershot, or wry mouth; brindle markings; overt aggression toward dogs or humans

early 19th century in Devon, England, by Parson John Russell. Reverend Russell was a fox hunting enthusiast who wanted a hunting companion that was small enough to comfortably enter and dig out a fox's den, while fast and fit enough to keep up with the horses. Russell began his breeding program with a number of local breeds, including Bull Terriers, Beagles, the Black-and-Tan Terrier, and the now-extinct Old English White Terrier.

This self-assured breed is best described as alert and thrives on adventure and activity. This can be handled by a long walk and some vigorous play each day, making the

Parson Russell Terriers occur in two coat varieties, smooth (left) and broken-coated (right).

The Parson Russell is first and foremost a working terrier—the less glamour the better.

Parson Russell suitable for apartment living if attention is given to daily exercise and stimulation. It is less scrappy toward strange dogs than many other terriers, but it will definitely want to chase any cat or rodent that should come in sight. An unneutered male may believe itself capable of anything and will often be aggressive toward dogs many times its size.

The Parson makes a loving companion, devoted to its family. It may be too active for infants, but can play well with children three years of age or older. Obedience training from an early age is a must. Strong-willed and easily bored, this terrier may not make an eager student, so keep the training sessions short and fun and seek the advice of a profes-sional trainer if it shows any signs of nipping. It makes a fine watchdog, as it barks only when alerted.

When given access to a yard, it will chase anything that moves, explore any holes it may find, and dig wherever a scent takes it, so gardeners beware. The tail of the Parson Russell is docked to about 4 inches (10.5 cm) to provide the owner with "a good handhold," which may be needed to extricate it from a hole once it has cornered a raccoon or fox.

The Parson Russell Terrier is long-lived, with a typical life span of 13 to 15 years. The breed has few health problems, although it has shown a slight genetic tendency toward Legg-Perthes disease, cataracts, and other eye problems. Litters generally contain four to eight puppies and whelping is usually uncomplicated. Grooming requirements are minimal (a weekly brushing is a good idea to remove loose hairs and teach some self-discipline at the same time).

The Jack Russell Terrier was accepted as the American Kennel Club's 145th breed, and the breed name was officially changed to Parson Russell Terrier in 2003 at the request of the national breed club.

Schnauzer, Miniature

The Miniature Schnauzer is the most popular breed assigned to the Terrier Group by the American Ken-

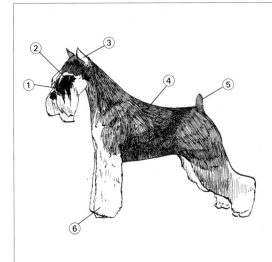

Illustrated Standard

① Head strong, rectangular, and long

② Eyes small, oval, and deep set

③ Ears set high; carried erect and pointed if cropped; if uncropped, small and V-shaped, folding close to the skull

④ Topline straight, slopes slightly down

⑤ Tail set high and carried erect, docked just long enough to be visible over backline

⑥ Cat feet

❏ **Color:** salt and pepper, black and silver, or black

❏ **DQ:** under 12″ or over 14″, white except for small white spot permitted on chest of black dogs (white not to be confused with silver white under throat and chest)

The Miniature Schnauzer is the only breed in the Terrier Group with no ties to the British Isles.

The black Miniature Schnauzer is a dog of tremendous style.

nel Club and is, in fact, one of the most popular of all recognized breeds. Unlike most terriers, the Miniature Schnauzer does not hail from the British Isles. It is German in origin, having descended from the larger Standard Schnauzer. The theory is that the small size of the Miniature Schnauzer was arrived at through crossings with Affenpinschers during the formative years of the breed.

Today there are three distinct schnauzer breeds: the Standard, Miniature, and Giant. All three share a working dog heritage, with the Miniature especially adept as a ratter and stable dog. The Miniature is a courageous dog, but less aggressive and quarrelsome than most terriers, including its larger namesakes. It is also less prone to the high-strung antics regarded as typical of the terriers.

In the home, the Miniature Schnauzer has proven itself to be outgoing, well-mannered, and personable. It gets along with people of all ages, and is notably long on patience with the antics of children. This breed dislikes extended separations from its master, and would prefer to travel along rather than be left behind. Unlike many terriers, it is tolerant of other animals in the home and rarely involves itself in fights or shows of aggression. Its exercise requirements are not extensive, although regular workouts are advised to keep the dog in optimal physical condition. It thrives in all types of environments and households.

The Miniature Schnauzer is one of the most intelligent terriers and has had good success in mastering the rigors of competitive obedience training. As with all headstrong breeds, a basic amount of obedience training is advised even if you have no intention of competing.

In appearance, the Miniature Schnauzer is a compact, stocky dog standing 12 to 14 inches (31–36 cm) in height and weighing approximately 15 pounds (6.8 kg). Its distinctive facial look is derived from regular groomings to shape the whiskers and bushy eyebrows that are characteristic of the breed. It sports a double coat, with a hard, wiry outer coat and a close undercoat.

The typical color is salt and pepper in shades of gray. To retain the correct texture for show competition, the coat must be regularly plucked and stripped. Owners of pet-quality Miniatures often prefer to go the easier route and have the coat clipped (usually three or four times a year) to keep the dog looking tidy.

The Miniature Schnauzer is normally quite healthy, with an average life span of 13 to 15 years, but a number of health problems occasionally affect this breed. Breeding stock should be evaluated and deemed clear of the presence of progressive retinal atrophy and congenital cataracts. There are also instances of bladder, kidney, and liver disorders. The Miniature Schnauzer is also susceptible to periodontal disease, so attention should be given to mouth hygiene.

Although very rare, a few cases of a new, deadly disease called mycobacterium avium infection have been found in a few dog breeds, including the Miniature Schnauzer. This infection is similar to tuberculosis and is spread by contact with infected bird droppings or contaminated water. This infection is hard to diagnose, with symptoms being diarrhea, vomiting, weakness, loss of appetite, and extremely swollen lymph nodes. The lymph nodes are the primary point of infection, and a misdiagnosis of lymphatic cancer may be made.

Litters average from three to six puppies, with the offspring born darker than they will appear as adults. The tail is docked quite short, so that it is just visible over the topline of the body when erect. The ears of the Miniature Schnauzer are often cropped, although there has been a trend in recent years toward uncropped ears.

Schnauzer, Standard

This breed hails from Germany and dates to the 16th century. Although it is classified by the AKC as a member of the Working Group, its original purpose was in the terrier tradition: rat catcher and home guard. The Standard Schnauzer has also been used for police and war dispatch duty.

The Standard Schnauzer's coat can be salt and pepper, as here, or solid black.

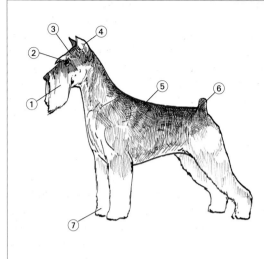

Illustrated Standard

1. Expression alert and spirited
2. Eyes oval with long eyebrows, which should not impair vision
3. Head strong, rectangular, and long
4. Ears set high; carried erect if cropped; V-shaped and mobile so they break at skull level if uncropped
5. Topline slopes slightly down
6. Tail carried erect and docked from 1 to 2″
7. Feet small, round, compact

❏ **Color:** pepper and salt or pure black
❏ **DQ:** males under 18″ or over 20″; females under 17″ or over 19″

The Standard Schnauzer is the oldest of the three Schnauzer breeds.

The Standard Schnauzer is not quite as game and challenging as many terrier breeds, but it is very inquisitive, energetic, and eager to please. It has proven itself to be both a fit worker, doing such chores as guard work and retrieving, and a very loving, loyal companion.

The Standard Schnauzer is a medium-sized dog with a square build, harsh coat, docked tail, and ears that are often cropped. It is a very hardy breed with few health problems other than a slight tendency toward hip dysplasia. It takes naturally and eagerly to obedience training and competition, which is a good outlet for its abundant energy and an antidote for its stubborn streak.

The Standard Schnauzer is a good pet for active people who can devote the needed time to the dog's exercise and discipline training. This breed needs a lot of attention and considers itself an integral part of the family. Its sensitivity to sight and sound make it a natural watchdog. If taught adequate self-control, it will usually get along peacefully with other animals and children, but it can be aggressive, especially to other male dogs. It does not take well to confinement or long periods alone, and may exhibit its frustration in destructive ways.

The Standard Schnauzer has a harsh, wiry outer coat and a soft undercoat that must be brushed regularly and professionally trimmed several times a year to maintain a tidy appearance. Unruly hairs are generally plucked out with the fin- gers or a stripping comb, and the whiskers about the face are scissored to maintain the proper appearance. The coat should not be shaved or clipped extensively, as this will affect the texture of the outer coat, which provides protection for the skin. Skin exposure often leads to irritations and sensitivities.

A litter of Standard Schnauzers usually contains from four to nine puppies. Most bitches make excellent, attentive mothers who may become irritated if the litter is given too much human attention in the early days. The Standard Schnauzer has the least tendency toward genetic disease of the three Schnauzers. It is generally very long-lived, averaging 13 to 15 years. While much less common than in the Giant, hip dysplasia can be found in the breed, as well as epilepsy and hypothyroidism.

Schnauzer, Giant

The Giant Schnauzer is well named—it is a giant among dogs. It ranges from 23 to 27 inches (58.4–68.6 cm) in height and can weigh close to 100 pounds (45.4 kg). It is assigned to the Working Group by the American Kennel Club, as it was originally bred to work with cattle, but among its ancestors were some terrier strains. The breed originated in Germany, where three Schnauzer lines developed.

The Standard Schnauzer is considered to be the original ancestor of the line, and crosses with Bouvier

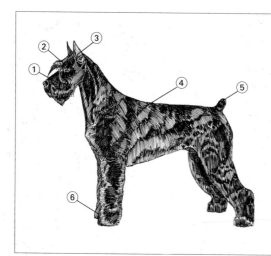

Illustrated Standard

① Rectangular head
② Oval deep-set eyes
③ Ears may be cropped or uncropped; when uncropped, ears are V-shaped
④ Short, straight back
⑤ Tail docked to second or third joint, carried high
⑥ Cat feet

❏ **Color:** solid black or pepper and salt
❏ **DQ:** overshot or undershot, markings other than specified

The Giant Schnauzer was one of the breeds used to produce the Black Russian Terrier.

des Flandres and Great Danes were introduced to enhance size and strength.

The Giant Schnauzer requires adequate space for movement and vigorous exercise, and does best in a household with a large yard and with owners that have time to devote to the needs of a working dog. It is naturally protective of house and home, and often a bit standoffish with strangers. The Giant breed does best in a one-dog family, as it may be threatening to other housepets.

The breed's dense, double coat is wiry to the touch. A daily combing and brushing will generally keep it looking tidy, but stray hairs will need to be plucked out regularly. Attaining the sculptured beard and eyebrows that are characteristic of the breed generally requires a professional's touch.

The Giant Schnauzer gets along well with children as well as adults, but its play is very enthusiastic and may be a little too rough for small children. The sheer size and strength of the breed makes obedience training a must, as an unruly Giant would be intolerable.

With an average life span of 12 to 15 years, this breed is long-lived for a dog of this size. However, like many of the largest breeds, the Giant Schnauzer has a tendency toward hip dysplasia. It is estimated that nearly 15 percent of the breed has borderline to severe dysplasia. Breeding partners should always be x-rayed and certified clear of the problem before mating. There are

The Giant Schnauzer should be evaluated for hip dysplasia at age two.

also rare incidences of hypothyroidism and epilepsy. The number of puppies in a litter generally ranges from five to eight.

Scottish Terrier

The Scottish Terrier, commonly known as the "Scottie," typifies the "Scottish type": a long-bodied, low-slung, prick-eared terrier with a rough coat and fearless disposition. The breed has long inhabited Scotland's craggy mainland and is thought to have descended from the various working terrier strains that were common in the Highlands and also figured in the formation of the West Highland White, Dandie Dinmont, Cairn, and Skye Terriers.

From earliest times, the Scottish Terrier was never limited to the tradi-

The Scottish Terrier is one of the most familiar dog breeds. Brave and devoted to its owner, it is a true global favorite.

tional ratting function associated with most terriers, but also served as a hunting companion. Despite its size, the Scottie proved to be adept at retrieving from land and water and was used in various gundog capacities.

The breed is extremely well fixed in type and temperament. The Scottie stands 10 to 11 inches (25.4–28.0

Illustrated Standard

1. Long skull, of medium width
2. Small, almond-shaped eyes
3. Small, prick ears, pointed
4. Uncut tail, about 7″ long, carried with a slight curve but not over the back
5. Legs, short and heavy boned

❏ **Color:** black, wheaten, or brindle of any color
❏ **DQ:** none

cm) in height and weighs from 18 to 21 pounds (8.2–9.5 kg). The outer coat is very harsh and wiry, and the undercoat is quite dense. The tail is not docked and is carried upright. The overall impression is of a compact, well-muscled dog that packs a lot of strength into a small frame.

The Scottie is affectionate and playful toward its master, but it is every bit the game terrier when strangers or other dogs are involved. It will take on any dog, regardless of size, that invades its territory. While it can be good-natured and extremely tolerant of the antics of the children that share its household, it can be cold or even belligerent with anyone unfamiliar. It prefers to be a one-master dog. These qualities make Scotties able watchdogs, but the breed is not for everyone. A suitable owner must be willing to match wits with the stubbornness of this intelligent, self-confident dog and enforce some disciplinary guidelines. Obedience training and adequate vigorous exercise are highly recommended.

The Scottie's characteristic trim requires several trips to the grooming parlor each year, although interested fanciers can master the trimming techniques for a pet if guided by an experienced hand. Grooming for show involves plucking and limited trimming to retain the required harshness and flow of the

Scottish Terriers have been the companions of at least two American Presidents: Franklin D. Roosevelt and George W. Bush.

coat. The coat should be brushed thoroughly every second day to prevent matting.

The breed is generally quite hardy and often lives to 14 or 15 years of age. Kidney stones can be a problem. The breed has a slight genetic tendency toward von Willebrand's disease, Cushing's syndrome, hypothyroidism, epilepsy, liver shunts, and juvenile cataracts. The most common genetic disorder is termed "Scottie cramp," in which an afflicted dog will have difficulty walking steadily under situations of extreme stress or excitement. This is not life threatening and usually abates as soon as the dog calms down. Litters generally contain three to five puppies who quickly show great bone and a dense coat. Puppy socialization is especially important

with the Scottie, as it can develop a sharp disposition if not shown a lot of affection while young.

Sealyham Terrier

The Sealyham Terrier originates from Wales in the 19th century, where it was utilized as a hunter of such cunning animals as foxes, weasels, and ferrets. This gives an indication of the courage of the breed, as it would fearlessly pursue and attack any predator. The Sealyham boasts a determination and eagerness for the hunt that is unsurpassed.

A variety of breeds is thought to figure in the Sealyham's background, including the White English Terrier, the Fox Terrier, the Dandie Dinmont, and the Bull Terrier. The breed has endured through the years as a result of the efforts of sportsmen; it did not gain much attention as a show dog until the early part of the 1920s.

The characteristics of the breed include its white, wiry double coat, button ears, heavy eyebrows and whiskers, and short coupled body. It stands approximately 10½ inches (27 cm) in height and weighs 22 to 24 pounds (10.0–10.9 kg). The tail is docked and carried upright.

The Sealyham coat requires frequent trips to the groomer and considerable routine care to keep it looking tidy. Proper technique requires unruly hairs to be plucked; this requires a skilled hand. To prevent the coat from matting, it must be thoroughly combed through several times a week. The Sealyham also requires more bathing than is typical of other terriers, as its white coat

The Sealyham Terrier is a native of Wales and came into being in the latter part of the 19th century.

comes in frequent contact with the ground and easily picks up and shows dirt.

The Sealyham Terrier is generally well behaved in the home, and shows a distinctive sense of humor in its play. It retains a very youthful nature no matter what age it may be. It is most suited to a home with adults that can pay it a good deal of attention and allow it some vigorous exercise. A Sealyham is wary and suspicious of strangers, but not prone to aggressive outbursts. These characteristics make it a natural watchdog—alert enough to recognize danger yet not bothersome with noisy outbursts at every unusual sound. It is, however, the embodiment of spunk, so a good dose of discipline is required to counterbalance this dominant personality. Some Sealyhams can be antagonistic toward unfamiliar dogs, especially males.

Gameness is an essential ingredient in the personality of the Sealyham Terrier.

Like many of the all-white breeds, the Sealyham is sometimes prone to deafness and eye problems. Otherwise, it is quite long-lived with a life

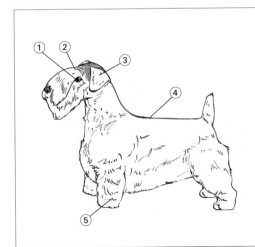

Illustrated Standard

① Medium-sized, oval, deep-set eyes
② Long, broad, powerful head
③ Ears folded level with top of head, rounded tips
④ Topline level
⑤ Feet large and round

❑ **Color:** all white, or with lemon, tan, or badger markings
❑ **DQ:** none

span of up to 15 years. Litters generally contain from three to six puppies, which become very animated at a young age. Obedience training from early on is suggested.

Silky Terrier

The Silky Terrier is another toy breed with a terrier heritage. It hails from Sydney, Australia, where it was derived from matings of Yorkshire Terriers and Australian Terriers. The breed was originally known as the Sydney Silky and was often used to

From this headstudy, the Silky's relationship to the Yorkshire is unmistakable.

clear mice and rats from farmers' fields. The Silky quickly gained popularity, as it sported the soft, lustrous coat of the Yorkie (but with little of the grooming requirements) yet maintained the true terrier spirit in a compact body.

Today the Silky Terrier is assigned to the Toy Group, but don't let such a designation fool you. It is based primarily on size, not on temperament, for the Silky could easily be placed in the Terrier Group for all its spunk, energy, and overall gameness. This Toy breed does not take naturally to the life of a pampered lapdog, although it certainly loves affection and attention. The Silky has a dominant personality and will try to take control of its environment if the owner is not wise to this tendency. Obedience training from an early age is suggested.

The Silky is extremely protective of its home and master, perhaps taking this tendency a bit too far at times. While it makes a wonderful watchdog, the Silky Terrier tends to be a noisy, sometimes argumentative breed that does not care to share its home with other pets unless they are introduced early in life. The Silky can get along amicably with children, if they are taught not to play roughly. This dog also has a natural desire to dart after any small animal it may spy, so it is advisable always to use a leash outdoors when the dog is not in a fenced area.

The Silky Terrier is normally a healthy, rather long-lived dog, with a

The Silky Terrier comes from Australia and resulted from crossings between imported Yorkshire Terriers and resident Australian Terriers. This Toy breed retains its terrier spirit.

life span of 12 to 15 years. It is susceptible to some disorders common in many toy breeds: dislocations of the kneecap or elbow, Legg-Perthes disease (hips), diabetes, and epilepsy. The Silky dam has fewer whelping problems than other toys and produces litters that normally

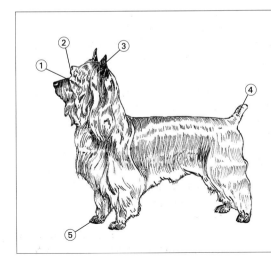

Illustrated Standard

① Small, almond-shaped eyes
② Flat skull with shallow stop
③ Small, V-shaped, erect ears
④ Docked tail carried high
⑤ Small cat feet

❑ **Color:** blue and tan
❑ **DQ:** none

average three to five puppies. The puppies should be monitored for possible tooth problems while growing. The Silkies usually mature at around 18 to 24 months of age.

While not nearly as troublesome as the Yorkie's, the coat of the Silky Terrier will still need some grooming to keep it in good condition. To avoid matting, a daily brushing is strongly suggested. This moderate amount of work will help to foster the glossy coat that gives the breed its name and distinctive appearance.

Skye Terrier

The Skye Terrier is one of the oldest "Scottish-type" terriers; the breed is thought to date back to the 16th century, if not earlier. The breed originated on the Isle of Skye, where farmers bred them from among their best working stock for destroying underground vermin.

It is very long in body, while standing only 10 inches (25.4 cm) at the shoulder. The Skye Terrier is, in fact, twice as long as it is high and is best described as a big dog on short legs. It is covered with a profuse coat parted to fall straight down on either side of the body, while covering much of the face.

The coat is one of the most notable breed characteristics. It is double, with a soft, wooly undercoat and a hard, flat outer coat that reaches at least 5½ inches (14 cm) in length. It must be one color overall, but may have varying shades of the same color throughout the coat. Permissible colors are black, gray,

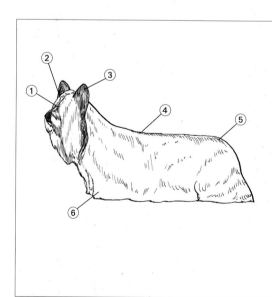

Illustrated Standard

① Medium-sized, close-set eyes
② Head long and powerful
③ Ears, if prick: placed high, held erect; if drop: larger and set lower
④ Topline level
⑤ Tail long, well-feathered, preferably carried no higher than backline
⑥ Large hare feet

❏ **Color:** black, blue, gray, silver, fawn, or cream, preferably with black ears, muzzle, and tail tip. Adult color may not be present until 18 months.
❏ **DQ:** dudley, flesh colored, or brown nose

The Skye Terrier combines glamour with true terrier temperament.

blue, silver, cream, or fawn, and the ears are invariably black. Its legs are quite short and muscular, and it sports a long, well-feathered tail. Its ears can be either pricked or dropped.

The coat requires daily care if it is to reach its full potential. While it requires little or no trimming, it must be brushed and combed each day to prevent snarls, and requires frequent touch up baths, since it picks up dirt as it brushes against the ground during movement. Most of the dirt is easily shed, however. A metal comb and a pin brush are most suited to the task. The hair

One of the oldest of the terriers, there are written references to the Skye Terrier dating back to the 16th century.

around the mouth and rectum also needs frequent attention to remove all debris that can cling to the area.

In temperament, the Skye Terrier is quite feisty and stubborn. While it can be extremely devoted to its master and even tolerant of children if raised with them, it can also be quite aggressive with outsiders. It is an avid watchdog and tends to be a bit noisy. The Skye Terrier can be snappy when meeting other dogs and requires a good amount of obedience instruction. It is best suited for adults in one-dog households who have the interest and patience to give the coat the extensive atten-

tion it requires. Its exercise requirements are not substantial. Because of its long body length it does not do well in cramped quarters or in homes that require the dog to climb a lot of stairs.

The Skye Terrier is a sturdy dog with good stamina and an average life span of 10 to 12 years. There is a tendency toward hypothyroidism and disc problems. Litters have a wide range, and have been known to contain up to ten puppies. Puppies are born with a coat that is lighter than the adult coloring. It will normally clear to proper shadings by 18 months of age.

The Soft Coated Wheaten Terrier came to the notice of dog lovers during the middle of the 20th century and was recognized by the AKC in 1973.

Soft Coated Wheaten Terrier

Southern Ireland is the homeland of the Soft Coated Wheaten. It is believed to be the oldest of the Irish terriers, dating back more than 200 years and a likely ancestor of the Kerry Blue Terrier. Despite its heritage, it was rarely seen in the United States until the 1940s, and it was recognized by the AKC in 1973. The breed owes its name to the ripe-wheat color of its coat. While this breed originally functioned as most other terriers in ridding the fields of small vermin, it also showed great ability as a sporting dog in the hunt and as a herder of cattle.

The Soft Coated Wheaten is a medium-sized dog, standing to 19 inches (48.3 cm) at the withers and

The Soft Coated Wheaten Terrier is an amiable breed that can hunt, herd livestock, guard the home, and warm the heart of all who love it.

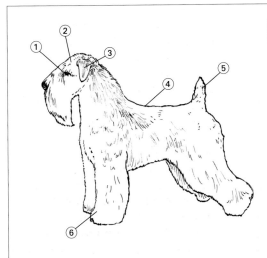

Illustrated Standard

1. Medium-sized, slightly almond-shaped eyes
2. Head appears rectangular, powerful
3. Ears fairly small, breaking level with skull
4. Back strong and level
5. Tail docked, carried gaily but not over back
6. Feet round

❑ **Color:** any shade of wheaten
❑ **DQ:** none

weighing between 35 to 45 pounds (15.9–20.4 kg). It has button ears, dark eyes, and a docked tail. The abundant, naturally wavy coat is the highlight of the breed. It is a clear wheaten color, soft in texture, and sheds little.

Unlike many of its terrier cousins, the Soft Coated Wheaten does not exhibit many aggressive tendencies, even toward other household pets. It gets along peacefully and cheerfully with everyone, and can be trusted to play alone with children. It is a quick and avid learner that rarely fails to cooperate with its owner's wishes. The breed thrives when allowed vigorous exercise, but can still be raised within the confines of a city or apartment. It is a people-oriented breed that does not do well when confined alone for long stretches of time. Several walks a day will suffice to keep the dog in good trim, but do not keep a Wheaten outside for long lengths of time during very warm weather, as it does not tolerate the heat well. It is a natural watchdog, but not prone to continuous barking.

The Wheaten's coat requires a great deal of attention but it should not be extensively trimmed. For show purposes, it can be tidied with thinning shears, but clipping, plucking, and styling are not allowed. To avoid snarls, the coat should be combed through at least every other day with a wide-toothed metal comb and a slicker brush that will not rip out the hairs.

The profuse coat of the Wheaten may sometimes mask skin allergies, but otherwise it is a healthy breed. Life expectancy is 12 to 15 years. There is a rare genetic predisposition to protein-wasting disease in this breed. Wheaten dams have few whelping problems, and litters generally contain five or more puppies. The newborns will be born with coats that are darker than the adult shade, but this will usually be resolved by 18 to 24 months of age.

Staffordshire Bull Terrier

The Staffordshire Bull Terrier, along with its larger cousin, the American Staffordshire Terrier, finds itself in the unenviable position of having to defend itself against a public image of a crazed "pit bull terrier." This image does not do justice to a breed that is, in fact, very affectionate and intelligent. Well-bred, well-trained Staffordshire Bull Terriers are not synonymous with the vicious creatures commonly termed "pit bulls." Such unfortunate animals are almost always the products of improper mixed breedings (using the most vicious parents possible) and improper training (being deprived of honest affection and discipline). Many are *taught* to be mean.

The Staffordshire Bull Terrier hails from the Staffordshire region of northern England, where, in ages long since past, large, muscular dogs of more than 100 pounds were regularly used in the "sport" of dogfighting. Over time, these early relatives of today's Mastiff and Bulldog were gradually downsized through selective breeding. Dogfighting reached a peak in the mid-19th century when crosses with working terrier strains were introduced to give the resulting dogs greater speed and agility. The result was a Staffordshire Bull Terrier—35 pounds (15.9 kg) of sheer courage, tenacity, and an extremely punishing bite.

This "sport" was eventually outlawed and breeders discovered that by raising this dog with discipline and affection rather than instruction in viciousness, it became a very personable canine associate. Over the years the Staffordshire Bull Terrier has proven itself to be an extremely loyal, affectionate breed that is quite popular as a companion in the home. A Staffordshire Terrier that has been raised with an ample amount of obedience training and affection will be

Muscular and sturdy, the Staffordshire Bull Terrier is a progenitor of the American Staffordshire Terrier.

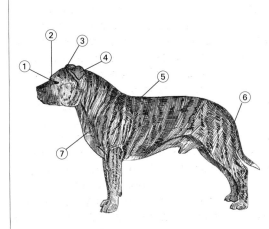

Illustrated Standard

1. Medium-sized, round eyes
2. Distinct stop, short foreface
3. Head short, deep, broad skull, pronounced cheek muscles
4. Ears rose or half prick, not large
5. Level topline
6. Tail medium length, carried low
7. Wide front

❏ **Color:** red, fawn, white, black, or blue, solid or with white; any shade of brindle or brindle with white
❏ **DQ:** black and tan or liver color

The Staffordshire Bull Terrier was once a fighting dog in the British midlands. Today it is England's favorite terrier breed.

very devoted and gentle toward its master. Its effectiveness as a watchdog is superb.

Today's Staffordshire Bull Terrier is an extremely muscular breed that imparts an immediate impression of strength and power. It has a long, undocked tail and a smooth coat, which can be found in a variety of colors. It stands approximately 16 inches (41 cm) at the shoulder and weighs 24 to 34 pounds (10.9–15.4 kg).

This breed is generally hardy and healthy, with a life span of 10 to 15 years. As with other powerful breeds, cases of hip dysplasia have been reported. The breed has been prone to cataracts, but this genetic disorder has become rare due to the elimination of affected dogs in breeding. Litters generally contain five or more puppies.

People considering owning this breed have a responsibility to give it ample exercise and obedience training. It should not be allowed to roam free. This breed does not get along well with other pets in the household.

Welsh Terrier

As the name implies, the homeland of the Welsh Terrier is Wales. This very old breed has been kept

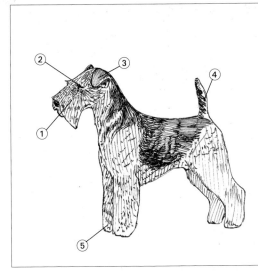

Illustrated Standard

1. Head rectangular
2. Small, almond-shaped eyes
3. Small, V-shaped ears, folding just above level of skull
4. Tail carried upright, docked to level of occiput
5. Small cat feet

❏ **Color:** deep tan with black or grizzle jacket
❏ **DQ:** none

true to type for at least 100 years. The effect of earlier crosses of the Old English Terrier, as it was originally known, with the Wire Fox Terrier produced a compact, medium-sized dog of great stamina and intelligence, capable of hunting the fox, otter, or badger.

The Welsh Terrier stands about 15 inches (38.4 cm) at the withers and weighs approximately 20 pounds (44 kg). Its coat is hard, wiry, and very abundant. The color is a rich black and tan. Its tail is docked to a medium length and is carried upright. The ears are folded just above the top of the skull.

The personality of the Welsh Terrier is very well rounded, having the inborn spunk and tenacity of the typical terrier but lacking much of the aggressiveness. It gets along agreeably with everyone—including other dogs—and has a natural desire to please. It will never shy away from a challenge, however, as it is extremely courageous.

Welsh Terriers are sensible, trainable, and wonderful pets for both town and country.

The Welsh Terrier is one of the oldest of the terriers and is thought to be in the background of several similar breeds.

The Welsh takes obedience instruction with a more positive attitude than many of the more stubborn terriers. The breed's intelligence is apparent in any task it undertakes, and it has had considerable success in obedience competition.

In the home, the Welsh Terrier is a fine, loyal companion that is trustworthy around children. While not overly vocal, it is instinctively attentive to all that goes on around it and is a natural watchdog. It is clean and does not need much grooming. Regular brushing and the plucking of stray hairs will generally keep the coat neat, while the typical facial expression is achieved through some careful trimming. An experienced breeder or groomer can teach the interested fancier how to achieve the desired look at home.

Welsh Terriers are quite hardy, but the breed has a slightly higher incidence of allergic skin conditions, epilepsy, thyroid problems, and glaucoma than many terrier breeds. The normal litter size is from three to six puppies.

West Highland White Terrier

The West Highland White Terrier has been present throughout Scotland for hundreds of years. It traces back to the native terrier stock that also served as ancestor of the Scottish, Dandie Dinmont, Cairn, and Skye Terriers. The "Westie," as it is commonly known, had the perfect conformation for work among the hills and crevices of the Scottish Highlands. Its compact body allowed it to go to the earth after its prey, and it was nimble enough to navigate the rocks while trailing after a fox, badger, or otter. It demonstrated a natural cunning and intelligence unsurpassed by the other terrier breeds.

The striking white coat of the Westie, as contrasted with its jet black nose, is the breed's most notable trait. The harsh double coat grows to about 2 inches (5.1 cm) in

West Highlands have distinguished themselves as show dogs and in all manner of competitive performance events. "Westies" are good at what they do and they seem to know it.

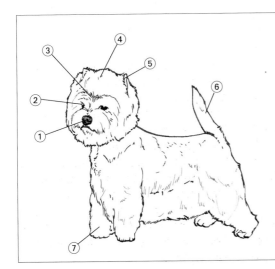

Illustrated Standard

1. Muzzle blunt
2. Medium-sized, almond-shaped eyes
3. Stop defined
4. Head appears round
5. Small, erect, pointed ears
6. Relatively short, carrot-shaped tail, carried gaily but not over back
7. Feet round

❑ **Color:** white
❑ **DQ:** none

The West Highland White Terrier is a close relative of the Cairn Terrier and is much sought after as a pet and companion.

length. There is an abundance of hair on the face. Despite its color, the coat is not overly difficult to maintain, since a hard coat easily releases dirt. The coat should be thoroughly combed every other day and routinely trimmed around the edges to keep the ends tidy. A Westie destined for the show ring requires expert grooming and trimming, but owners of pet Westies can attend to their needs by clipping or shaping with scissors. This will soften up the desired harsh outer coat texture, however, and make it less susceptible to retaining dirt.

The Westie packs a lot of terrier into a small frame, as it stands only 10 to 11 inches (25.4–28.0 cm) at the withers and weighs approximately 18 to 19 pounds (8.2–8.6

kg). Its legs are slightly longer than the other "Scottish type" terriers. Its penetrating dark eyes and erect ears help give the breed an especially keen expression.

With an average life expectancy of 13 to 16 years, the Westie has proven itself to be a robust terrier. It is prone to some allergic skin disorders, and an elevated incidence of deafness. Owners should also be on the lookout for signs of pain in the hips or jaws, as inflammation in these areas can become chronic. The average litter size is three to five puppies.

A rare, ultimately fatal, genetic disease known as globoid cell leukodystrophy is present in some West Highland White Terrier lines. This is a recessive disease that affects the brain. It can be carried by dogs not manifesting the disease, so it is important that all Westie sires and dams be tested for this mutation before breeding.

Temperamentally, the Westie makes a fine companion in home or apartment, suitable for all ages except very young children. It is affectionate and playful; it will peacefully tolerate the presence of other animals in the house, but probably not be enthusiastic about this. It is a natural watchdog, and may carry this to an extreme by being *too* vocal. If confined for any length of time, it may also react with tireless barking. This can be controlled if corrected while young. The Westie is also an avid digger; this is a natural instinct that is hard to control. Its stamina enables it to keep pace with the most avid outdoorsman, and ample exercise is advisable. Be sure to have deep-set

fencing in your Westie's outside area, as it is a renowned escape artist.

Yorkshire Terrier

This diminutive member of the Toy Group can trace its heritage to various terrier strains common to Scotland and England in the 19th century. Despite its small stature, the breed can be as perservering and feisty as any of its larger relations. The Yorkie was originally known as the Scottish Terrier, a name which was shed once the breed became the favorite of the coal miners in the Yorkshire area. There these dogs, used to rid the mine shafts of mice and other small vermin, earned a reputation for being steadfast, dependable workers.

The Yorkshire Terrier is currently the most popular toy breed, usually ranking around sixth in popularity

Illustrated Standard

1. Medium-sized eyes
2. Small, V-shaped ears, carried erect
3. Small head, rather flat on top
4. Level topline
5. Tail docked to a medium length and carried slightly higher than the level of back
6. Round feet

❏ **Color:** blue and tan. Yorkshire Terriers are born black, gradually attaining their blue and tan coloration as they mature.

❏ **DQ:** none

Its coat is the Yorkshire Terrier show dog's crowning glory.

among all 150 breeds, owing largely to its lustrous, silky coat and charming personality. When properly maintained, the coat can grow to beyond floor length. This regal appearance has made it a popular, fashionable pet. Fashion is not without a price, however. The Yorkie's coat requires vigilant, daily attention to reach its potential. Owners that prefer to keep the hair short often choose a "puppy" or "schnauzer" cut by a professional groomer. Those Yorkshire Terriers destined for the show ring will require constant monitoring for potential damage to the coat and will generally require that the coat be kept in wrappers.

The Yorkshire Terrier enjoys the life of lapdog and can be extremely affectionate toward its master. It will get along well with other housepets, but flourishes best when allowed to "rule the roost." The typical Yorkie makes a fine watchdog, with a keen sense of hearing, a lively bark, and above average intelligence.

Most Yorkshire Terriers weigh 2 to 7 pounds (0.9–3.2 kg). Because of this tiny, compact body many Yorkie bitches are too small to whelp puppies naturally, making them likely candidates for cesarean sections and life-threatening births.

The average litter size is two to four, with all the puppies being born black with tan markings. As the puppy grows, the black hairs will be shed and replaced by the straight, silky, steel-blue or tan hairs that are the highlight of the breed. The Yorkie is slow to mature and will take at least two years to attain its adult stature.

Since the breed is generally quite active around the house, little formal exercise is needed. Although most

Yorkies are not unusually frail, it is best not to expose these dogs to the extremes of the various seasons— be it the heat of summer or the cold of winter. To accomplish this, some owners keep their Yorkie paper-trained throughout its life.

A small stature brings with it some obvious dangers. First, bone fractures can easily result if a Yorkie suffers a serious fall or is stepped on. Second, the breed cannot easily defend itself should it be attacked by larger dogs.

Prospective buyers should not be drawn to Yorkies described as "teacup" size, as very tiny dogs often have health problems throughout life. An increased number of skull malformations and open fontanellas have been found in Yorkies less than 8 inches (20.3 cm) in height. The breed is also prone to patellar luxation, eye irritations, Legg-Perthes disease, spine problems, and often does not react well to anesthesia. Liver shunts are a congenital problem found in some Yorkshire Terrier lines. Afflicted puppies have improper blood supply to the liver, which impacts liver function, slows growth, and may lead to death if untreated. Surgery is required to correct the problem, and it is hoped that this malady will be all but eliminated eventually by not breeding to lines that pass on this tendency.

Yorkshire Terriers have a high incidence of tooth decay and should be fed a primarily dry diet. Brushing their teeth daily is advised (if the dog cooperates), as is regular scaling of plaque by a veterinarian.

It should never be forgotten that a terrier heritage is basic to the Yorkshire Terrier. It can be an extremely assertive breed, determined to have its own way. This strong will is often enhanced by owners who treat the Yorkie more like a pampered child than a dog—constantly carrying it, grooming it, and habitually doting on its care. If left unchecked, the dog's willfulness can result in destructive behavior when the Yorkie is left unattended. A moderate dose of obedience training will do much to temper the will of the Yorkshire Terrier and mold it into a superior housepet.

The Yorkshire Terrier was developed by relocated Scottish weavers during the latter half of the 19th century. The earliest specimens were far larger than today's Yorkshires.

Useful Addresses and Literature

Registries

American Kennel Club
5580 Centerview Drive
Raleigh, NC 27606-3390
(919) 233-9767
Website: *www.akc.org*

The Canadian Kennel Club
89 Skyway Avenue, Suite 100
Etobicoke, Ontario
Canada M9W 6R4
(416) 75-5511

Books

Bonham, Margaret. *Soft Coated Wheaten Terriers*. Barron's Educational Series, Inc., Hauppauge, NY: 2005.

Bulanda, Susan. *Boston Terriers.* Barron's Educational Series, Inc., Hauppauge, NY: 2002.

Coile, D. Caroline. *Encyclopedia of Dog Breeds.* Barron's Educational Series, Inc., Hauppauge, NY: 2005.

Coile, D. Caroline. *The Jack Russell Terrier Handbook*. Barron's Educational Series, Inc., Hauppauge, NY: 2000.

Coile, D. Caroline. *The Yorkshire Terrier Handbook*. Barron's Educational Series, Inc., Hauppauge, NY: 2004.

Frye, Fredric. *Schnauzers*. Barron's Educational Series, Inc., Hauppauge, NY: 2002.

Lehman, Patricia. *Cairn Terriers*. Barron's Educational Series, Inc., Hauppauge, NY: 1999.

Miner, Dorothy M. *Airedale Terriers*. Barron's Educational Series, Inc., Hauppauge, NY: 1998.

Rice, Dan. *West Highland White Terriers.* Barron's Educational Series, Inc., Hauppauge, NY: 2002.

Stahlkuppe, Joe. *American Pit Bulls*. Barron's Educational Series, Inc., Hauppauge, NY: 2000.

Vanderlip, Sharon. *Fox Terriers*. Barron's Educational Series, Inc., Hauppauge, NY: 2001.

Vanderlip, Sharon. *Scottish Terriers*. Barron's Educational Series, Inc., Hauppauge, NY: 2001.

Cairn Terrier.

Australian Terrier.

West Highland White Terriers.

Magazines

The American Kennel Club Gazette
260 Madison Avenue
New York, NY 10016

Dog Fancy
Subscription Division
P.O. Box 53264
Boulder, CO 80323-3264

Justteriers
P.O. Box 518
Trappe, MD 21673

National Parent Clubs for the Terrier Breeds

Anyone interested in securing information about any of the breeds included in this book are advised to contact the applicable parent club through the American Kennel Club web site listed on page 161. All the clubs support educational initiatives and most publish their own magazines and educational material.

Index